SPRINT CAR RACING

AMERICA'S SPORT

SPRINT CAR RACING
AMERICA'S SPORT

Bill Holder
Foreword by Brad Doty

Howell Press

SPRINT CAR RACING
AMERICA'S SPORT

Bill Holder
Foreword by Brad Doty

Designed by Theresa Munt

Edited by Keri Moser, Ross A. Howell, Jr., and Jamie L. Bronner

Library of Congress Cataloging-in-Publication Data

Holder, Bill.
      Sprint car racing : America's sport / Bill Holder
      p. cm.
      ISBN: 1-57427-064-8

      1. Automobile racing.   2. Sprint cars.   I. Title.

GV1029.S67H65 1997   796.7'2
                        QBI97-41555

Printed in Hong Kong
Published by Howell Press, Inc.
1713–2D Allied Street
Charlottesville, VA 22903
(804) 977-4006
http://www.howellpress.com
10 9 8 7 6 5 4 3 2 1

Dedicated to Henry Meyer, a sprint car pioneer

A portion of the profits from this book will be donated to
the Dayton Auto Racing Fan Club Injured Drivers Fund.

Table of Contents

Opposite: Superstar Steve Kinser at speed. (Phil Kunz)

Foreword

As a former driver and still a huge sprint car fan, I may be accused of being partial to this type of racing. In my opinion, there is no other form of racing that will excite you and get your blood flowing like watching a pack of fire-breathing, open wheel, winged sprint cars bounce through a corner only inches apart, at over a hundred miles per hour.

There are those who will argue that non-winged sprint car racing is better than the winged type, or that dirt is better than pavement.

With sprint cars, you can have any of those combinations, and you can bet that it will always be a heck of a show.

The majority of you who read this book are most likely already sprint car fans. The rest of you surely will be by the time you have finished it.

Brad Doty
Television announcer and former sprint car driver

Opposite: Frankie Kerr (23S), Johnny Herrera (4A), Tim Engler (73), and Joe Gaerte (9TW) power down to the start of a World of Outlaws race at Eldora Speedway. (Bob Fairman)

Left: Brad Doty. (Bill Holder)

Sprint Car Thoughts

The sprint car began as a non-winged, no-roll-cage car that ran on very narrow tires and was built from the ground up by the mechanic and crew. It was a demanding sport both physically and mentally for the driver, on tracks that could be very rough, with equipment that was sometimes questionable. It had to be a very precise effort on the driver's part to stay out of trouble and be running at the end of the race. It didn't take much to put a car out of the race.

Today, it has become a very technical sport with almost all equipment purchased from a professional builder. The cars have become very fast and lightweight, which is very demanding on the drivers. The tracks have become "smoother" because of the wide tires and the large wings. The drivers have to be mentally alert all the time during the race.

Sprint car racing is a very exciting sport to watch with the features mostly being of the fifteen- and twenty-mile length, which means that every driver is going for it from the start. Sprint car drivers that have moved to other types of racing have proven they can drive any type of race car after driving the sprinters.

Rollie Beale
Retired Supervisor, USAC Sprint Car Division
Former USAC Sprint Car Champion

When you love the sport of sprint car racing, it can easily consume your whole life. No thrill compares to the rush you get from the combination of the smell, the noise, and the action on the track.

After forty years as a participant, I can still feel the thrill! I wouldn't trade the special moments in sprint car racing for anything—the fun we've had with the drivers and knowing we've provided some great thrills for the fans. I'll do everything in my power to keep sprint car racing alive into the next century, so the next generation can "feel the thunder."

Bert Emick
President, All Star Circuit of Champions

Opposite: The excitement of non-winged sprint car racing is illustrated by this flurry of action during a race at the Terre Haute Action Track in 1991. Bill Rose (6) leads Jack Hewitt (63) in the 1991 USAC Terre Haute Classic. (Randy Jones)

Sprint car racing is one of the fastest growing sports in the United States. Long one of the most down-to-earth sports, its recent strides in the electronic media have made it even more fan-accessible. Not only can fans at the track visit their favorite drivers before and after the races, they can also communicate with them via the Internet's World Wide Web on a regular basis. Fans unable to attend the races have access to more and more sprint car races on television, too.

The demand for coverage of the sport in the print and electronic media has increased dramatically in recent years. Since the Associated Press started covering sprint car racing on a regular basis, more and more daily newspapers are hiring racing columnists. Radio stations often invite drivers to appear on their fan call-in shows, too.

With the increase in television coverage, more major corporations are turning to sprint car racing with their marketing dollars. In years past, sprint car series and cars were rarely sponsored by businesses outside the auto industry. Today, manufacturers of everything from water purification products to land-moving equipment are sponsors.

It wasn't long ago that sprint car racing was perceived as the minor leagues for the stock and Indy car ranks. Not anymore. Due to the increase in television coverage, sponsorship, and event purses, fewer drivers are leaving the sport. They're also building long-term relationships with car owners and crew chiefs rather than jumping from team to team.

So, while sprint racing has grown into a booming business, the appeal of the fire-breathing, mud-slinging cars and their drivers is stronger and more widespread than ever before.

Richard Day
World of Outlaws

Opposite: Locked to the ground, this sprinter is on the move. (David Tucker)

Left: The method of moving a sprint car team has evolved from a simple flatbed trailer to an awesome semi-hauler like that of World of Outlaws driver Jac Haudenschild. (Phil Kunz)

Below: Dave Darland in motion at USAC Lawrenceburg in 1993. (Randy Jones)

Sprint car racing has withstood the test of time and gotten better with age.

Today's high-horsepower machines strongly resemble their ancestors of fifty to sixty years ago. Although there have been tremendous advances in safety measures, the sprint car technology—four wheels, a small frame and body, a high-powered engine, and a simple chassis setup—remains the same.

Perhaps because of this simple technology, NASA engineers are not needed to set up a sprint car, and sprint car racing continues to increase in popularity.

The attraction could also be the thrill of driving such a creation, with your back inches in front of the fuel tank, your feet inches behind a 700-plus HP engine, and your butt inches above the driveline... all in a vehicle so lightweight that the slightest misdirection could literally send you flying.

A lot of this could also be the reason sprint car racing is so popular among the fans—the simplicity, the speed and power, and, to be realistic, the danger.

However, probably the most popular aspect for the fans is the close competition. The maneuverability of these race cars allows their drivers to race within inches of each other on a lap-after-lap basis, constantly exchanging positions, running side by side, and keeping most of the spectators standing throughout the short "sprint" races.

Following a sprint car race, many of the racers and spectators may appear winded, probably because they've held their breath throughout the contest.

No longer a regional sport concentrated in Pennsylvania, the Midwest, and California, sprint car racing is spreading across the U.S., even into "stock car country"—the Southeast.

The appeal and growth of sprint car racing parallel the appeal and growth of NASCAR Winston Cup racing, which has skyrocketed in recent years, attracting blanket television coverage and major corporate backing. Only sprint car racing approaches the popularity of NASCAR in the marketing of souvenirs, memorabilia, and collectibles.

Sprint car racing now has its own National Hall of Fame and Museum, along with several publications that focus largely, if not exclusively, on the sport.

With the television exposure of sprint car racing increasing, plus the involvement of major corporations, the sport can do nothing but continue to grow in popularity.

Wayne Kindness
Editor, Sprint Car News

Opposite: Californian Steve Kent puts the pedal down to take advantage of the huge downforce provided by the car's pair of wings. (Phil Kunz)

Introduction

It all begins with a low rumble, the sound of power waiting to be unleashed. It's a thumping, throbbing sound that seems to build the excitement of what is to come!

Then, a green flag is dropped from the starter's stand, and suddenly a new world of excitement descends. Instantaneously, 800 HP power plants come to life, driving the machines forward at huge speeds and accelerations. Driver and machine become one as the combination of steel and flesh devours straightaways in mere seconds. Huge rear tires paw at the dirt surface, clawing for every bit of traction.

The massive aluminum wings are doing their work, squatting the cars down, keeping them running straight and true. The cars round the track without the driver ever lifting his foot off the throttle. This is really "pedal to the metal" all the way around!

It's been stated that these cars really attack all the senses when they're at speed. First, there's the screaming sound of the engines that fills the eardrums and sends pulsing ripples through every one of your body's muscles.

Your eyes tell you about the swirling dust that trails off the end of the cars, filling the air. There's also that characteristic smell of burning alcohol. This is certainly no place to wear your Sunday best; you'll most likely be covered with a layer of Mother Earth, to the point where there's even a gritty feel to your tongue. Ears, eyes, nose, and throat—these cars get them all, but true fans wouldn't have it any other way.

This amazing phenomenon is created by the magnificent racing machines known as SPRINT CARS. As any fan who has ever seen them run knows, these awesome machines provide the fastest and most exciting racing in the land.

But it must be quickly noted that we're NOT talking about machines that run on the two-and-a-half-mile ribbons at Daytona or Indianapolis. This is more down-to-earth racing that is done mostly on short dirt ovals dotted across the U.S., many times on little backwoods tracks that were carved out by their owners. They are tracks that draw vast crowds who come to see their heroes do battle at breakneck speed. They are also tracks that sometimes have ruts and holes that can grab a sprint car and hurl it high into the air, or into a series of death-defying spirals down the track. Also, there are a number of short paved tracks that host mostly non-winged sprint cars.

Even though the sprint cars run on shorter tracks, danger rolls with them every time they are pushed out for action. Death and serious injury are a part of the scenario, and every driver is well aware of the risks he faces each time out. No wonder the sprint car drivers have been called the "Last American Heroes." The name is very appropriate.

In earlier times, sprint car racing was considered a gateway to the Indianapolis Motor Speedway, and a number of greats, like A.J. Foyt, Mario Andretti, Parnelli Jones, and Bobby Unser, used the sprints for that purpose.

One major difference between sprint racers and those who drive the NASCAR and Indy machines is that many of the sprint car drivers are part of the crew themselves, doing much of the work. Sometimes it's just a one- or two-man operation on a tight budget,

Opposite: One of the best in the winged sprint cars is Pennsylvania's Fred Rahmer, shown in the famous Apple Chevrolet car at speed in a mid-1990s competition. (Phil Kunz)

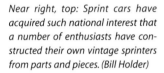

Near right, top: Sprint cars have acquired such national interest that a number of enthusiasts have constructed their own vintage sprinters from parts and pieces. (Bill Holder)

Near right, center: Sprint car racing isn't just jumping into the seat and getting pushed off. There's much work to do, and Pennsylvanian Ed Lynch, Jr. shows that the driver does much of it himself. (Bill Holder)

Near right, bottom: Superstar Jack Hewitt likes his sprint car racing the old way—without a wing overhead. Here he wins the sprint feature at Eldora 4-Crown Nationals. (Randy Jones)

Far right: One reason that Frankie Kerr is such a successful driver is that he knows what makes his car tick. (Larry Reese)

Opposite: Dave Blaney drove this car for a number of World of Outlaws seasons, winning the championship in 1996. Here he is in 1994. (Phil Kunz)

Top right: Many of the famous old sprint cars have been recovered and restored. This restored car maintains the charisma of its glory days. (Eric Thompson)

Bottom right: Al Unser, Jr., one of Indy car racing's most famous drivers, got his start in this sprint car. (Eric Thompson)

Opposite: USAC sprint racer Doug Kalitta does a little "rock 'n' roll" with his left front wheel kicked up off the track at USAC Terre Haute in 1992. Jack Hewitt is in the background. (Randy Jones)

Below: The words lettered on this sprint car exemplify the spirit of most of these fearless drivers. (Phil Kunz)

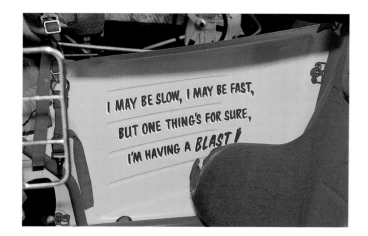

so it's not surprising to see a driver pull into the pits and jump under the car to help change a failing rear end.

The appearance of these interesting racing machines is really a combination of the past and present. First, there's the classic curving body design that was such a part of the racing scene before the advent of the rear-engine Indy cars in the mid-1960s. Quite frankly, the look of sprint cars really hasn't changed much through the years, with one major exception: that large aluminum wing mounted atop some cars, the purpose of which might not be obvious to the new fan.

The wing is used for what is called "downforce." In other words, the rushing air pushes down on the wing and keeps the race car firmly attached to the track. Cars with these wings are capable of much greater speed than the few non-winged cars that still run in the 1990s. A number of sprint car purists find great fault with this aerodynamic enhancement, calling it a crutch for the driver since it keeps the car from sliding in the turns.

A majority of racing with the winged cars is done on the dirt, while the more traditional non-winged cars hold about half of their races on dirt and half on pavement. Each style of racing has its own, very dedicated fans. A non-winged fan wouldn't usually attend a winged race, and vice versa.

Sprint car racing is an increasingly popular motorsport, with interest really growing in the 1990s. Every year the sport enjoys more TV coverage, with a number of the big events now receiving live national coverage. It can't help but continue to grow as more and more people view the unbelievable excitement of the open wheel cars.

Another indicator of the growth of the sport can be seen on the toy counter, where models of most of the sport's big stars appear. Not only are the little kids enjoying the models, but they have become collectibles for the bigger kids, the fans themselves, as well. The values of some of the models have escalated to four or five times their original price.

It should be noted that the sprint cars of today have evolved over most of this century. For those who want to relive the days of old with sprints, a number of groups across the country stage events in which restored, old-time sprint cars are brought back on the track.

If you want to see the history of sprint car racing up close, there are a number of excellent museums, such as the Antique Auto and Race Car Museum in Bedford, Indiana, and the National Sprint Car Hall of Fame and Museum at Knoxville (Iowa) Speedway.

Several national publications have covered sprint car racing, including *Sprint Car News,* which was totally dedicated to sprint cars, and *Open Wheel* magazine, which provides heavy sprint car coverage.

So that's an overview of sprint car racing, a sport with an exciting past and an even more exciting future, as technology makes the cars faster and faster. It's the purpose of this book to make you a fan. So buckle up tight—it's going to be a heck of a ride!

Opposite: Different drivers negotiate a turn on a high-banked track in different ways. The center car has its tires cocked to the right with the rear end coming around, while the front car has its tires straight. (Phil Kunz)

Sprint Car Roots

It might be hard to believe, but you can trace the beginnings of sprint car racing back a full century. In fact, the first open wheel oval track race is believed to have taken place in Cranston, Rhode Island, in 1896. Through the decades, the sprint car as we know it today has evolved through many different shapes and names.

In the early part of this century, where to race the powerful machines became a problem. Then promoters realized that there was a very logical answer looking them right in the eye: fairgrounds' horse racing tracks! These ovals were perfect for the various open wheel car types. Tracks were converted by the hundreds for a different and louder type of horsepower. Today, a number of these tracks are still active, the most famous being Knoxville (Iowa) Speedway, which holds the famous Knoxville Nationals, one of the sport's premier events.

In 1915, a group of fairground promoters got together and formed an open wheel sanctioning body, the International Motor Contest Association (IMCA). The American Automobile Association (AAA) was also sanctioning open events at the time. It's interesting that AAA considered any racing done outside its jurisdiction "outlaw," a term that would stay with the sport to this day. In fact, the premier sprint car sanctioning body of the 1990s, the World of Outlaws, still uses the nomenclature.

One of the early influences on the sprint car was the Speedster, which used main components from the Ford Model T. Initially two-seaters, the cars were eventually narrowed to single-seaters. These configurations evolved into what became known as Big Cars, the direct forerunners of today's sprint car design.

There were other early influences as well. One example is the larger Championship Cars, which eventually became the Indy cars we know today. In appearance, these cars looked much more like the classic sprint cars, but they were about ten inches longer and had a larger tail tank for the hundred-mile races they ran.

Others point to the influence of the smaller midgets, which externally resembled the sprint cars almost identically. Still, most agree that the Big Cars, which strongly resembled today's sprints, are the direct ancestors of the modern sprint racers. Whatever its origin, today's car did come to fruition, and its many thousands of fans are certainly glad that it did.

Because Ford racing parts were so widely available during the 1920s, there was a huge Ford influence on those early Big Cars. The biggest change to the stock Ford power plants came with the addition of powerful cylinder racing heads, which allowed these engines to compete with the pure racing engines of the era. The most famous of the new racing heads were the popular Fronty Heads, which turned the Ford into a powerhouse capable of competing with the pure racing Miller engines of the time.

In the mid-1930s, the engine of choice was the famous four-cylinder pure racing Offenhauser engine. The power plant affectionately became known as the Offy, and acquiring one of these legendary engines today is an extremely expensive venture.

The exciting and very dangerous Big Car sport gained popularity in the 1930s and led to the establishment of two new sanctioning bodies: the American Racing Association (ARA), on the

Opposite: For many, the 1960s were the golden years of sprint car racing. Here, Johnny Rutherford (9) and Roger McCluskey (51) were on the pole, coming down for the green flag in a 1965 USAC race. (Ken Coles)

Overleaf left: The classic lines of this early sprint car have been retained in the design of modern machines. (John Farquhar)

Overleaf right: Early sprint cars were characterized by long exhaust pipes that traversed the length of the cars. (John Farquhar)

West Coast, and the Central States Racing Association (CSRA), which was based in the Midwest.

There are some interesting stories about hybrid sprint cars that came from other types of cars. There are stories of Championship Cars being shortened by ten inches into sprint cars. Famous sprint car builder Henry Meyer recalled running both sprint and champ races with the same car by adding or removing frame inserts.

There are also stories about midgets that were turned into sprint cars by extending their frames. These hybrid sprinters were sometimes recognizable by their small tail, which was actually the midget tail that remained on the "new sprint."

During the early years of sprint car racing, every car was built by hand, so not one of them was exactly the same as another. The cars were built to last; it was not unheard of for a sprinter to hang around in active competition for two or even three decades, passing from owner to owner, changing colors and numbers, and being modified and updated through the years. These old cars still turn up once in a while in deserted barns or garages and are excellent candidates for restoration.

In the late 1970s, the age of manufactured sprinters began. It continues today, with companies actually assembling complete cars or kits. Built extremely light, these cars don't have the durability of their predecessors, so many of them don't make it past a single season. Bad crashes mean they'll be discarded rather than rebuilt. Hence, many of the cars of current famous drivers no longer exist and unfortunately won't be around for future generations of race fans.

Top right: The fact that the history of this vintage sprinter is unknown doesn't lessen its attraction. This car was restored by a loving owner and is shown at vintage open wheel meets. (John Farquhar)

Center right: A number of former Indy roadsters were converted into sprint cars with outstanding results on paved tracks. USAC decided they had an unfair advantage and barred them from competition. (Phil Kunz)

Bottom right: Nostalgia for the 1930s is still alive in the 1990s, as evidenced by this field of restored sprinters at a vintage open wheel show. (John Farquhar)

Opposite: The old fairground where this classic sprinter was photographed at one time supported overflow crowds. Some fairground tracks still host sprint car racing. (John Farquhar)

Opposite: This 1930s sprint car was probably built in a backyard. It carries a Plymouth four-cylinder engine and was hand-molded from car body parts. (Bill Holder)

Top left: The powerful Offenhauser engine was the power plant of choice during the 1940s and 1950s. (John Farquhar)

Bottom left: The twin carburetors of this vintage sprint car protrude through the side panels of the lower hood. Multiple carbs were common during this era, with some engines sporting three two-barrel versions. (John Farquhar)

Below: Wire wheels might be the classic look of today, but in the 1930s, they were standard fare. (John Farquhar)

Overleaf left: Sammy Sessions (83), in his Rufus Greys car, and Greg Weld (93), in his Don Brown–built roadster, battle at Queen City Speedway near Cincinnati in 1969. Note the early roll cages on the cars. (Ken Coles)

Overleaf right: One of the most famous sprint cars in history is the Iddings Car built by Henry Meyer. The car was powered by an Offenhauser power plant and competed in the Championship Car ranks, setting many records on paved short tracks in the Midwest. (John Farquhar)

Right: Built in the late 1960s, this #21 sprinter was one of the first cars to run with the All Star Circuit of Champions series. The car was powered by a 350-cubic-inch V-8 engine. (Phil Kunz)

Opposite: This #2 sprint car was a terror in the 1940s and 1950s, when it was wheeled to perfection by the great "Spider" Webb. (John Farquhar)

As things change, the more they seem to stay the same with sprint cars. Why change success? With the sprints, that has certainly been the attitude. The car shape has stayed basically the same over the years. Certainly modern technology has had its hand in the engines, tires, and suspension, but that classic shape is still recognizable.

One thing that has changed is the amount of protection afforded the driver of a sprint car. The early sprinters were dangerous, very dangerous! A rollover crash couldn't help but cause injury to the driver since there was no overhead protection of any kind. None! During the 1950s, a roll bar was installed on the tail, directly behind the driver's head, but this was only a marginal

improvement. It wasn't until the late 1960s that complete roll cages came along and greatly reduced the number of serious injuries.

Following the demise of AAA's sponsorship of racing in the mid-1950s, a new organization was formed, the United States Auto Club (USAC), which would become dominant during the 1960s and 1970s. Many of its stars moved on to Indy Cars. Such names as Johnny Rutherford, Bobby Unser, Mario Andretti, Don Branson, Gordon Johncock, Parnelli Jones, and others monopolized sprint car racing during the early-to-mid-1960s, followed by Gary Bettenhausen, Rollie Beale, Larry Dickson, Pancho Carter, Sheldon Kinser, and on and on.

Would you believe that NASCAR actually had a sprint car division?

Right: Note the stout curving front axle and cross spring front suspension of these 1960s-style sprint cars. Later sprint cars would use torsion bars and coil-over shocks. (Ken Coles)

Opposite: Shown are the two types of USAC sprint cars raced during the 1970s. Examples are the rear-engine machine (52) of Greg Weld and the standard upright machine of Benny Rapp (34). The rear-engine cars would later be barred. (Ken Coles)

Right: Jud Larsen was a real dirt mover, shown here churning up the track at Terre Haute, Indiana, in 1965. (Ken Coles)

Above: Jan Opperman runs in the famous Speedway Car, shown here at the 1976 USAC Hulman Classic, which he won. (Ken Coles)

Left: Indy star Tom Sneva, in 1974, drove this roadster creation, Carl Gelhousen's car, after the rear-engine cars were banned from running USAC. Note that it still bears the look of a rear-engine car. (Ken Coles)

For two years (1952 and 1953), the Bill France organization fielded the open wheel cars. The sprint cars never caught on, though, and NASCAR moved back to an exclusive stock car circuit.

A significant happening during the late 1960s was the introduction of a small number of rear-engine sprinters that ran only on the pavement with USAC. With its sleeker shape and superior handling, the design definitely had an unfair advantage over the traditional sprinters. Only teams with a great deal of money could afford the rear-engine sprinters, and they were so much faster than the other cars that they were barred after only one year. One driver, though, who made his name in those cars was Tom Sneva, who would go on to Indy car glory.

A big change that came around the start of the 1970s was the introduction of overhead and hood-mounted wings to the age-old shape, a move that was not universally applauded. Many argued that the use of such massive aerodynamics took the driver out of the equation and that the wings served as a crutch. Others argued for the greater safety provided during a rollover.

The winged cars also brought forth a new breed of drivers who would become known as "outlaws." These mavericks weren't associated with any particular team. In 1970, though, under the genius of Bud Miller, a number of these drivers organized under the label of the All Star Circuit of Champions. Such names as Rick Ferkel, Jan Opperman, Bobby Allen, Lou Blaney, and Tommy Quarterson put on super exciting one hundred–lap races. After a brief lull mid-decade, the All Star name reappeared in the late 1970s. The series continues today.

In 1978, another winged group appeared when Ted Johnson organized his now-famous World of Outlaws. Through the years, the group has received considerable publicity through the exploits of its stars, such as the superlative Steve Kinser, Sammy Swindell,

and Doug Wolfgang; and, in the 1980s, Dave Blaney, Jac Haudenschild, Jeff Swindell, Andy Hillenburg, Joe Gaerte, Danny Lasoski, and Stevie Smith. The key to the World of Outlaws's success is its travels all over the country—many of its teams carry national sponsors and benefit from national TV coverage. A number of participants in the group have become household names.

Throughout the 1980s, as interest in the sport grew tremendously, many new sprint organizations were formed. A majority of the racing was done with wings, but several organizations remained faithful to the old wingless ways.

The point should be made that sprint car racing is popular in other countries besides the U.S., including Australia, New Zealand, and Canada. Because the seasons are reversed down under relative to North America, many American drivers spend a portion of the year competing in Australia and New Zealand. All of the equipment used in these races comes from the U.S., and fans elsewhere keep close track of sprint car news in this country.

Unlike the situation for stock cars, the rules for sprint cars have remained pretty much the same across organizations. As a result, a driver can race throughout the U.S. without having to change his car.

In recent years, the most significant change to the sprint game has been the introduction of cars with smaller engines. Economy is the main reason for their invention; these cheaper engines allow more teams to participate in the sport.

As sprint car racing bears down on the next century, you can guess that the classic shape that came into being so many years ago will be retained. But you can also bet that the cars will get faster and more powerful, thrilling future fans as much as they have thrilled fans of the past.

Opposite: Californian Hank Henry was one of the renowned sprint car builders. This is a restored version of one of his cars. Famous drivers who drove his roadsters included Parnelli Jones, Jim Hurtubise, and Roger McCluskey. (Bill Holder)

Below: Ted Johnson brought sprint car racing to the national front with his World of Outlaws series in the late 1960s. His winged series now gets exposure on national TV. (Phil Kunz)

Sprint Car Technology

There it sits, quietly. With that huge wing looking much like a sunshade, it's hard to imagine the fury this car can wreak when it's brought to life.

For those unfamiliar with this sport, the modern sprint car looks strange and ungainly in its static mode. But those who have seen these machines at work know that every part of this mauler contributes to its ability to get around a dirt track faster than any other type of race car.

As mentioned earlier, there's still a bit of the past embedded in the modern sprint car. It's in the outer body shell only, though. That vintage shape from the 1920s is still basically in place. The classic look includes a long, engine-containing front hood that rests just ahead of the driver's office, where his knees are practically pushing up against the firewall, and the curved, shapely rear tail, which contains the necessary alcohol fuel supply.

Today, in the search for lighter and faster cars (current sprint cars weigh only about 1,300 lbs or less), some body pieces are constructed of light but strong fiberglass. In the earlier days, the cars were all steel and aluminum. In fact, during the 1930s, fenders from passenger cars were often beaten into shape to serve as hoods and tails. The modern sprint car is held together by a stout chrome molybdenum steel frame of which the roll cage is an integral part.

And then there are those giant wings attached to the top of the roll cage, twenty-five-square-foot aluminum slabs that perform a number of important functions. Of course, not all modern sprint cars carry the overhead metal, but in the 1990s, about eighty percent or more use them. Interestingly, when wings first came into being, they were fabricated from plywood. Even so, they proved to be somewhat effective; the flowing air certainly didn't know the difference.

A winged sprint car actually carries two wings. There is the five-by-five-foot top wing and the hood-mounted two-by-three-foot front wing. The smaller wing doesn't get much attention, but it certainly deserves mention. Like the larger top wing, this appendage has vertical sideboards on its ends to keep the air contained over the wing surface while the car is at speed. In the case of sprint cars, that's BIG speed! The purpose, therefore, of the smaller wing is to push the front end of the car down and aid in tracking it in the desired direction.

Then, there's the massive top wing. When operating at full tilt, the wing pushes the car down with hundreds of pounds of force, really planting it firmly on the track. Any sliding is almost totally eliminated. It looks as smooth as driving on pavement, where the tires really are hooked to the track, but winged drivers will tell you that there is still some slippage.

The top wing is mounted on a slider device so that it can be moved by a hydraulic system that changes the aerodynamic characteristics of the wing. These changes can be made by the driver at top speeds.

As you can probably imagine, not having those wings topside, as demanded by several national sanctioning bodies, brings about an entirely different driving experience. With the downforce, as it is called, gone, driving is more in the hands of the

Opposite: These sprint cars, shown in Jacksonville in 1987, carry a twenty-five-square-foot aluminum wing that provides hundreds of pounds of downforce, keeping the car pressed hard to the track. (Phil Kunz)

driver. And although the cars are not running nearly as quickly, many think it's more exciting racing.

The big advantage of the wings, though, comes in cornering the car; they really glue those wide tires to the dirt and allow faster speeds through the turns. This phenomenon stems from the two large wing sideboards and the offset manner in which they are attached to the wing's center section.

With winged sprint cars, it's not surprising to see the drivers circle short tracks at full throttle, never lifting their right foot off the pedal. It's like some giant hand is holding that car to the track when all the laws of physics mandate that it should be flying into space. Power steering comes in really handy with these cars!

With that lack of slipping and maximum adherence to the track come amazing speeds. At the famous high-banked Eldora Speedway in Ohio, for example, the track record is 12.9 seconds, which equals an average speed of something like 135 MPH on a half-mile dirt track. On the straightaways, that speed has got to be approaching 160 MPH.

That enhanced speed is what the wing was originally conceived for, but two other interesting functions have come from it. The first and most important added advantage is the unexpected safety the overhead structure provides should the car roll over in a crash.

Because of the great speeds at which these cars run, a tremendous amount of energy must be dissipated in order to bring a rolling sprinter to a stop. A non-winged car tends to tumble for what seems like forever. That's where the advantage conferred by the wing

Opposite: Adhesion to the dirt track surface is greatly increased by super-wide treaded tires. Often, crews will cut additional treads by hand, depending on track conditions. (Bill Holder)

Left: Many different hood styles have appeared on sprint cars through the years. Note that Johnny Parsons's (55) hood features a slanted box design containing the fuel injection tubes. (John Mahoney)

BRODIX
McCREARY
SPARKS
7
BRADY
TRUCK EQUIPMENT
CO INC.
11
L
Mudd Off
BOWMAN
Motor Sports
PENNZOIL
WELD
WRIGHT
WELDING
ACE SHOCKS
BRADY
RAD
RACING TEAM
Larry
Pinegar
BRADY
TRUCK EQUIPMENT
CO. INC
EAGLE
GOODYEAR

Opposite: Locked tightly to the track by their wings, this pair of sprint cars, driven by Larry Pinegar and Rick Daugherty, duel at Jax Raceways in Jacksonville, Florida, in 1996. (Mark Funderberck)

Left: When a winged sprinter rolls upside-down and starts vaulting down the track, the wing helps to slow the car and lessen the force of the impact. (Eric Thompson)

comes in; as the sideboards crumple, they absorb energy and lessen the force of the impact on the driver. Rest assured; the wing isn't going to do any more downforce work after that rocking and rolling. But many drivers will quickly tell you that the wing has saved them from serious injury.

Finally, there's an economic value to the wing. With its large sideboards, there is a moving billboard coming by each person in the crowd every eighteen to twenty seconds. It should come as no surprise that the teams with big sponsors use every square inch of that space to substantial advantage!

So how is all that downforce on the car accepted at track level? Quite nicely—through four super-wide racing tires. The front tires are the narrower, obviously, since they are not doing any of the pushing; there's only rear-wheel drive here. Out back, there are sometimes as many as twenty inches of tire surface touching the track, really "putting the power down." The left rears are sometimes as wide as fifteen or sixteen inches, but the majority of the punishment is taken by the right rear. Hence, the wear rate is much greater on that tire, and it requires replacement much more often. Top-dollar teams often put on a new one for each feature race.

Crews have a lot of flexibility with the tires; they are able to vary the stagger (differences in diameter), the rubber compounds (harder or softer) used on a particular tire, the pattern of the tread, and the manufacturer (Goodyear, Hoosier, or McCreary). Many teams will "groove" a tire to meet specific track conditions or their driver's style.

Opposite: Driving close to other cars, as shown here at Kokomo (Indiana) Speedway, is a risky situation. Open wheel sprinters tend to catapult into the air when one car runs over another's wheels. (Randy Jones)

Top left: Wing experimentation has continued through the years. Check out the canted wing configuration on the left-hand car in this World of Outlaws competition at Tulsa, Oklahoma. (David Lawless)

Center left: Sammy Swindell's sprinter is rocked over going through a turn in a race at St. Augustine (Florida) Speedway in the 1990s. (Randy Jones)

Bottom left: By 1993, the amount of advertising and sponsor recognition on the wing sideboards was unbelievable. (Action Photos)

Top left: The heart of the sprint car is its ground-pounding engine, which must do much of its work in a blinding dust storm. Note the large filter on top of the injectors. (Bill Holder)

Bottom left: The right rear suspension of this modern sprint car shows the shock, rear axle, rear brake, and torque arm. (Bill Holder)

Top right: There are few Ford power plants and even fewer Chrysler engines in sprint car racing today. For the most part, it's a Chevy world. (Bill Holder)

Bottom right: Sprint car racers are always looking for better suspension systems. The way this coil-over shock is mounted shows one innovative technique. (Bill Holder)

Top left: The pits for a modern sprint car event are frantic places. It's every man for himself, with cars pulling in wherever there is room. (Phil Kunz)

Bottom left: This is the pit area at Bloomington (Indiana) Speedway during a winged sprint car race. (Eric Thompson)

Below: A crewman makes last-second preparations before this sprinter takes to the track. Notice the mounts that attach the wing to the top of the roll cage. (Eric Thompson)

Top right: The cockpit is a driver's operation center. A sturdy roll cage completely encircles the driver, who is buckled into a fitted race seat. Considerable hardware sits directly in front of him, including the power steering and fuel pumps. The drive-line runs directly under the driver. (Bill Holder)

Bottom right: A monster V-8 engine sits tightly between the front motor place and the front-mounted radiator. (Phil Kunz)

Opposite: This style of sprint car chassis is known as a "down-tube" design, in which tubes run from the top front of the roll cage to the front of the car. The arrangement stiffens the overall frame for greater safety. (Bill Holder)

Below: Visible is the tope rail, which starts its curve to accommodate the larger Shaver Ford Engine. (Phil Kunz)

Interestingly, these racing tires are only minimally inflated. Depending on conditions, the pressure ranges between three and five pounds. That's why many times you can see the tire walls flexing under the weight of the car.

Between the downforce of the wings, the power of the engine, and the tracking of the tires comes the suspension system, which must put it all together and make the car respond. These systems have evolved through the decades, starting out with a configuration that resembled the spring setup on horse-drawn buggies. This was called a "cross spring" because a large leaf spring was stretched over the axles, both front and rear. Later, torsion bars were substituted in the rear while the spring front was retained. Today, there are torsion bars on all four corners, which seems to be the best setup for maximum weight transfer.

There also have been attempts to utilize "coil-over" shocks, which incorporate both the spring and shock in a single unit. To date, that technique has not proven successful, although even some top teams have attempted it.

Finally, there is the probable most important part of the sprinter, the power plant that pushes it to heart-shaking speeds. Like other aspects of the cars, the power plant has come a long way. Initially, normal street engines were used, then pure racing engines, and, finally, the 410-cubic-inch, small-block fuel-injected killer engines of today. Sprint cars using this type of engine are often referred to as Super Sprints.

Would you believe that it's now possible to pull close to 2 HP per cubic inch with these pure racing aluminum power plants?

Many of today's engines are capable of exceeding the magic 800 HP level! No turbos or superchargers here; we're talking normally aspirated. Major sprint car engine manufacturers today include the likes of Gaerte, Shaver, Westfall, Donovan, Kriner, Kline, and Cornette. And these don't come cheap; top-of-the-line engines push the $35,000 figure!

And that's not all. To remain competitive, the engines have to be "freshened up" every so often. They're torn down and all of the parts cleaned and checked for wear or cracks. This is done as frequently as a team's pocketbook allows; top teams sometimes "freshen up" as often as every half dozen races.

There's no transmission on a sprint car, so it's necessary to get a push start to fire up the big power. "Push trucks" get behind the sprinters in the pits and push them up to 20 or 30 MPH—fast enough to fire up the engines. Starters have been considered, but cost and longtime tradition have kept this phase of the sport unchanged.

Finally, there's the quick-change differential, which enables crew members to change the gears in a matter of minutes when the car comes into the pits. Simply removing the rear plate, removing the gears, and inserting different ratio gears will hopefully increase speeds on the track.

Speaking of those costly engines, it should be mentioned that there is a growing class of sprint cars that use a smaller power plant, actually a 360-cubic-inch engine. These machines are called Limited Sprints and are a more economical way to race. Obviously, these cars are not as quick as their big brothers, being a second or two

Opposite: Check out the interior of this World of Outlaws transporter. There's storage space for the sprinter and enough equipment to do just about any repair. (Phil Kunz)

Top left: A view of the floor underneath the driver's feet. Shown are the torque tube, fuel pump, and throttle. (Phil Kunz)

Top right: A pair of quick-change rear ends lie in wait for future use. The protruding sections they are sitting on contain the rear end gears. (Phil Kunz)

Bottom: Side protection on a sprint car is provided by "nerf bars," which fill the space between the wheels to prevent another sprint car from getting into the body. (Phil Kunz)

slower than the 410-cubic-inch sprints, but the level of competition is still very exciting. The rules for Limited Sprints vary across the country. Many of the sanctioning groups don't allow exotic engine parts, and the wings are usually fixed in position instead of having the slider installed.

The Econo Sprint organization in Ohio has the right idea for getting the excitement of winged sprint car racing from a reasonable budget. The concept comes down to the fact that a number of aspects of the car are governed. First, there is the top wing, which is fixed; no slider here. Also, the front wing is removed entirely.

Econo Sprint cars use 305-cubic-inch steel block engines and three- to five-year-old sprinters—that really helps lower the cost of the sport. One Pennsylvania group uses tiny four-cylinder engines in its sprint cars. For many, such modifications haven't decreased the excitement level one bit!

Opposite: A growing trend in national sprint car activity is to race a more economical Limited Sprint. Externally, Limited Sprints appear the same, but they run on a smaller, 360-cubic-inch engine. (Phil Kunz)

Top left: Limited Sprints serve as a starting point for drivers like preteen Luke Castle from Ohio. He learned his trade while still in grade school! (Bill Holder)

Far left: An Econo Sprint, shown here racing at Fremont in 1990, is an economical Midwest sprinter that uses 305-cubic-inch engines and omits the front nose wing. (Phil Kunz)

Near left: For the beginning driver, the advantage of racing an Econo Sprint is definitely economical. It is possible to use an inexpensive engine and a used sprint car body. (Phil Kunz)

Driving with a Wing

Next to the thrill of watching a sprint car blaze around a short track, the most exciting association with one of these winged haulers is actually sitting behind the wheel. Ask any driver and you'll get an affirmative thumbs up!

Just looking at a winged sprinter is enough to make you wonder what it feels like, how it reacts when it's at flat-out speed. Even though everything looks pretty much soundly fixed on the car when it's just sitting there, that's certainly not the case. Dean Jacobs, who drives his sprinter in the All Star Circuit of Champions group, explains that three major adjustments can be made, depending on track conditions and driver preferences:

First, there is the stagger of the tires [the difference in circumference between right and left rear tires]. With a winged sprinter, we most times run with the right rear about fourteen inches bigger than the left. That seems to work for us pretty good. That's about twice as much stagger as we would put in a non-winged setup.

Then, there's the position of the overhead wing, which we can adjust. A rule of thumb as far as we're concerned is that the slicker the track, the farther back the wing is placed for traction.

Finally, we are able to adjust the torsion bars to optimize the configuration. Usually, we find that it works best when we tighten up the left rear bar. Sometimes we're right on, sometimes we miss it by a mile!

Ohio sprint driver Butch Schroeder explains that the faster you go, the more you feel the effects of that giant sunshade overhead. He notes that it's possible to change the location of the wing while at speed by using a control on the dash. "You want to have the wing in the full-back position on restarts so you will have maximum downforce for maximum traction."

Schroeder says that, even with the awesome downforce on the car, there is still some slipping when these winged warriors tear through the turns. "It happens more when the track is slicked up, but when it's tacky, you sure don't move around that much because the car is really locked to the track."

USAC sprint veteran Greg Staab says the feeling of driving a winged sprinter is that of stability and being planted on the track. "It's easier to make a move when you are committed to changing position on the track. But one thing you have to remember, because of the high speed you have going into a turn, once you commit to a particular line, you ARE definitely committed to holding that line."

With the huge speeds of the winged sprinters, the action is fast and furious. Staab explains that you need to look as far ahead on the track as possible and be alert for any trouble. "I try to watch for any abrupt movement in front of me that might indicate that somebody has lost control of his car. To avoid an accident, it's necessary to make a decision almost instantaneously. If you think about it, it's probably too late to take evasive action. For most drivers of these cars, it's an instinct action."

Opposite: World of Outlaws driver Johnny Herrera shows his stuff getting around a turn at Eldora Speedway. (Phil Kunz)

Moving around is something that Schroeder says he does when he's closely trailing another car at speed. "You can really feel the air as it comes off that car. The car jumps around a little, but when there is a car running alongside, you really don't feel any effect. The fact that the air is coming off the wing so high in the air lessens its effect."

Schroeder points out that, though it's small, the front wing plays an important part in stabilizing the car. "I lost a front wing once, and the front of the car sure gets a lot lighter. Even with it installed, the big power of the engine still has a tendency to pick up the front end on occasion."

The downforce of the winged sprinters also tends to make them paw harder at the track, bringing up more dust. With everything else these guys have to think about, there's also an occasional visibility problem. As Schroeder says, "There are times when you can't see more than a couple feet in front of you. Sometimes you just go into a cloud of dust and hope that there isn't another car hiding in there."

In addition to the dust particles, particles of considerably larger size imperil the drivers. Hard clots of clay and even harder rocks are kicked up from the track and occasionally pound the cars. Once in a while, a rock or clump of clay will get through the rock screen on the roll cage and give the driver quite a start. Schroeder says that what really gets your attention is getting hit on the fingers or hand by a rock traveling 100 MPH. Ouch!

And even if you're one of the sport's top drivers, sooner or later you're going to flip your race car. It happens no matter who you are, even to the likes of many-time World of Outlaws champion

Opposite: A head-on view of a winged sprint car at speed with the wheels cranked hard to the right. Note the dented leading edge of the front wing, which has to endure high-speed impacts of dirt clods and rocks during competition. (Phil Kunz)

Top left: Top competitors Dave Blaney (10) and Charlie Fisher (48) duel wheel-to-wheel at Eldora. (Eric Thompson)

Center left: With the tremendous torque available from their monster power plants, it's not uncommon to see sprinters raise their front wheels, as World of Outlaws regular Andy Hillenburg demonstrates in Haubstadt, Indiana, in 1997. (Eric Thompson)

Bottom left: Pedal down, these winged sprint cars, driven by Bobby Allen (1A) and Johnny Herrera (4A), try to find the quickest way around the Bloomington (Indiana) Speedway in April 1990. (Randy Jones)

Overleaf left: Stevie Smith (71) takes the low line under Sammy Swindell (1) in a blistering competition at Eldora Speedway in 1995. (Eric Thompson)

Inset: Joe Gaerte gets an unusual view from his sprinter at Bloomington Speedway in 1991. (Randy Jones)

Overleaf right: Jimmy Carr (65) and Sammy Swindell (1) pull "wheelies" in an attempt to take the lead at Haubstadt, Indiana. (Eric Thompson)

Right: It's quite a sight and sound to see twenty-four cars rumbling around together in four-wide, pre-race formation with their wings glinting in the sun and some 20,000 HP waiting to be unleashed. (Phil Kunz)

Bottom right: Joey Saldana is shown in a 1991 USAC sprint race at Kokomo Speedway. (Randy Jones)

Below: Ohio lawyer Tracy Hoover started his sprint car career in smaller open wheel Mini-Sprints but quickly caught on to winged sprints. (Phil Kunz)

Left: If you are not running at the front of the pack, the view is full of rocks, dirt clods, and blinding dust—this is definitely not the place to be! (Phil Kunz)

Below: The start of a winged sprint car race is a crowded situation. Here, it appears that there could be three different lines taken by these cars as they strive for the front-of-the-pack position. (Phil Kunz)

Steve Kinser. "It's a strange experience," Schroeder explains. "You're praying all the time when you're in the air that you will please land on your wheels. It's kind of strange, because it's really quiet when you are rolling through the air. But when you hit, it's really loud. You can really feel the wing cushioning the blow when you hit on it. It seems to slow you down, too, and get the ordeal over sooner. There are many times that you don't have any warning when a flip is coming."

Staab seconds those thoughts about the wing's cushioning effects but adds that it's a rather expensive way to slow down. "You can figure that you are going to wipe out a $550 wing along with the slide mechanism. When it's all over, you probably figure that it'll cost about a thousand dollars!"

Most drivers say that they are totally aware of who is running alongside them. As Staab explains, "You get to know the color of the cars. You also get to know the driving styles of the other drivers, which will sometimes dictate what your next move might be. When you're running alongside one of the big guns, it's a situation of not being intimidated."

Right: One complaint that old-time sprint car fans have about winged racing is that it's not as easy to see the drivers working in the cockpit. (MSPN)

Of course, there are also the 360 Limited Sprints and 305 Econos, which are gaining in popularity. Many drivers say that the winged 360 cars aren't much different from the full 410-cubic-inch sprints, especially on the shorter tracks. In fact, many drivers say that the 360-cubic-inch engine is better suited to the quarter-mile bull rings, where the awesome power of the 410s is just too much to be used.

Opposite: During the 1980s, USAC—which is now strictly a non-winged sprint organization—ran some races with winged configurations. This 1985 action shows a pair of USAC sprint cars closely tracking each other. (Phil Kunz)

Opposite, inset: During winter months in the United States, many sprint car drivers move their racing game to Australia. Here, in a pre-race ceremony, the flags of both countries are unfurled for the fans as the U.S. drivers get a huge welcome. (MSPN)

Left: One of the best in a winged sprint car was Rocky Hodges, who drove for the All Star Circuit of Champions series for a number of years, winning many races. (Phil Kunz)

Overleaf left: Jeff Swindell's sprinter is almost completely hidden behind Dean Lindsey's (2D) car in this 1995 competition at Eldora Speedway. (Eric Thompson)

Overleaf right: Dave Blaney, World of Outlaws champion in 1996, (10) takes the low line under Joey Saldana (77) in this race to the front at Eldora. (Eric Thompson)

WINGS ON PAVEMENT

We've talked about what it's like to drive a winged sprinter on dirt, but how about putting one of these machines on pavement? It isn't the most common thing (usually, sprinters run on pavement without wings), but it has been done. At least two sanctioning bodies run their winged sprints on pavement—the American Winged Outlaw Sprints (AWOL), in the southeastern part of the country, and the Ohio-based Econo Sprint organization.

The All Star Circuit of Champions was possibly the first group to try running on pavement, in the late 1980s. First and foremost, the All Stars wanted to see if the same dirt sprint cars could be used in this new application with only slight modifications. The organization didn't want its drivers creating special sprint cars for pavement.

These cars certainly weren't built with pavement in mind, though, so it was necessary to make some minor changes. Most of these were to the torsion bars and shocks; a bigger front axle also came into play. The cars were run low to the ground, too, and the wings mounted in the lowest possible position.

There was concern that the light chassis construction would not hold up to the increased stress of pavement racing, but that didn't prove to be a problem. There was some consideration given to degrading the engines, but that didn't turn out to be necessary either.

The cars were super fast. For example, at the paved Columbus (Ohio) Motor Speedway in the early 1990s, the track record for the speedy American Speed Association (ASA) stock cars was 14.56 seconds. Jeff Gordon, in his first effort in a pavement sprint car, turned the oval in 12.43 seconds—over two seconds faster!

Opposite: The driver of this #27 pavement sprinter raises considerable smoke trying to straighten out his car. (MSPN photos)

Top left: In a rare appearance of winged sprint cars on the pavement at Columbus Motor Speedway, Jack Hewitt takes the low line under Dave Fisher in 1989 action. (Bob Fairman)

Bottom left: In this paved action, the older roadster-style sprinter of Bob Seelman (74) gets past the machine of Rusty McClure (99) at Columbus during the first All Star race at the track. (Bob Fairman)

Driving without a Wing

Sprint cars without wings are physically very similar to their winged counterparts; the only real difference is the fact that those pieces of aluminum have been removed. Driving a sprint car without a wing is a world apart, but recall that it was the mode that produced sprint car racing's great early stars.

DRIVING WITHOUT A WING ON DIRT

Now we go from a world of down-pressing aerodynamics to a world in which the driver becomes a more significant factor in the outcome of a race on a dirt track. Greg Staab, a longtime USAC sprint driver, has driven the wingless machines for years and has some thoughts on how to make them run fast and efficiently:

> I really think that there is a lot more skill in driving without a wing. You are running out there right on the edge, just short of being out of control. Believe me, it's a fine edge to negotiate. One of the touchiest maneuvers you have to make is to make sure that the rear end doesn't pass you up when you're coming around the turns.

> I can feel when that is starting to happen. The logical thing to do is to let off the throttle, but that sometimes isn't the best thing to do. More often than not, more throttle will enable you to recover.

All Star veteran Kevin Huntley says that driving without a wing is easier for him. "It's a lot slower. With the wing, I'm running wide open, so this is pretty easy for me; you've got more time to correct mistakes."

Staab goes on to say that without a wing, the driver can get more of a feel for the track and be able to race on the best part of the track for his particular car's setup. For many non-winged racers, that's running up near the top of the track, against what is known as the "cushion," a buildup of dirt that provides a nice place to lean the right rear tire against.

It probably comes as no surprise that non-winged cars can function at their best with less power than their winged counterparts. With practically no downforce, less is more in the case of these machines. "With the winged sprint cars, most times the car with the best engine wins the race. That's not always the case with the non-winged cars," Staab emphasizes.

On the shorter dirt tracks, many drivers actually use 360-cubic-inch engines. It's a lot more efficient to use all of that lesser power than to spin away the extra horses of a more powerful 410-cubic-inch engine.

DRIVING WITHOUT A WING ON PAVEMENT

Smooth, smooth, smooth! That's definitely the required driving style with a wingless sprint car on pavement—no sudden jerks on the wheel, or you are one big marble. Staab says that you also need to be looking far ahead for any abrupt movements on the track that might indicate an accident. He continues, "You have to be a lot more concentrated driving these cars. When I approach a car from the rear, I study the line that car is taking so I will be able to make the pass."

Watching non-winged cars on dirt and then on pavement is about as different an experience as you can get. Where "loose-ness" is an attribute on the dirt—when the rear of the car tends

Opposite: During the 1960s, top-gun sprinters ran without wings. A.J. Foyt (2) passes Tony Bettenhausen, Sr. in tight non-winged racing at the 1960 Milwaukee Mile. Judging from the fact that Foyt's left front wheel is in the air, both are on the gas hard. (Ken Coles)

Overleaf left: Here, driver Kenny Rice illustrates the non-winged technique for turning right to go left on a dirt track. (Phil Kunz)

Overleaf right: You can see just about everything that is happening with the driver in a non-winged car and can gauge how hard he is working to keep the car moving toward the front. (Phil Kunz)

Opposite: A gaggle of non-winged sprint cars form up before doing battle in a USAC dirt race. Note the size of the massive right rear tires that will be clawing for traction once the cars get to speed. The stripes on the wall were cleaned off to show the drivers where the track ends and the wall begins. (Phil Kunz)

Top left: Doug Kalitta leads a pair of non-winged USAC sprint cars in furious action. (Phil Kunz)

Center left: Many times, the quickest way around a high-banked track is right up against the wall. (Phil Kunz)

Bottom left: Dave Darland is one of the best there is in a sprint car minus the gigantic overhead sunshade. Here, he's at speed at the Terre Haute Action Track. (Eric Thompson)

Below: Jack Hewitt, shown here at Winchester (Indiana) Speedway, is among the best at non-winged racing. His famous #63 ran up front for many years, and the veteran shows no signs of slowing down. (Randy Jones)

Top right: The late Rich Vogler would do anything it took to win. At Terre Haute in 1980, the legend lifts the left side of his non-winged sprint car, trying for an advantage on the track. (John Mahoney)

Below: Hang on! That would be the best advice as this non-winged sprint car stands on its tail during a scary flip. (Larry Reese)

Bottom right: Terry Shepard, shown here at Terre Haute, was one of many drivers to wheel the famous Hoffman Car from Cincinnati. (Eric Thompson)

Opposite: Tony Elliott of Kokomo, Indiana, is a longtime non-winged sprint car driver. Much of his success has been realized in this #17 car. (Eric Thompson)

Top right: Greg Leffler destroyed his car in this 1973 crash at the Indiana State Fairgrounds in Indianapolis. (John Mahoney)

Bottom right: Rich Vogler, in the #55 Elder Cadillac, looks at the track from a different angle as Dana Carter (in the black car) slides by in 1979 at the Indiana State Fairgrounds. (John Mahoney)

Below: Butch Winings emerged unscathed from this misadventure at Lincoln Park Speedway in Putnamville, Indiana, in 1995. (Kevin Horcher)

Top left: In one of the highest flights in a sprint car, Jackie Howerton sails over George Snider at Terre Haute in 1972. Notice that the back half of his tail is missing. (John Mahoney)

Bottom left: Tom Black takes a spill in 1996 at Lincoln Park Speedway. (Kevin Horcher)

Below, bottom: It might appear that this is a dirt sprint car crash, but that is not the case. A car has spun into the infield from its on-track crash and continued to do its "rock 'n' roll." (David Heithaus)

Below, top: Mayhem isn't limited to dirt racing, as George Snider illustrates in this 1975 crash at Winchester Speedway. It appears that the car is breaking into pieces as the tail bends upward from the impact. Paul Harrison is nearby the mishap. (John Mahoney)

Top left: Current NASCAR driver Tony Stewart drives the famous Glen Niebel #20 at the high-banked Salem (Indiana) Speedway in 1995. (Eric Thompson)

Bottom left: Speeds are scary for the powerful non-winged sprint cars on high-banked paved tracks. Here, a veteran USAC driver, Greg Staab, gets his machine through the middle of a turn at Salem in 1995 by keeping the car straight. (Eric Thompson)

Top right: Tom Bigelow's act literally falls apart above Don Nordhorn at Terre Haute in 1970. (John Mahoney)

Bottom right: The large offset of the right front tires on these wingless sprint cars is very evident. The arrangement allows for better cornering on pavement tracks. (Phil Kunz)

Left: The crew gains easy access to the engine compartment by removing the hood of this non-winged pavement sprinter. (Phil Kunz)

Overleaf left: Kenny Irwin, Jr. is one of many great NASCAR drivers who got his start in the sprints. Here he is at Salem in 1995. (Eric Thompson)

Overleaf right: There's no time to converse with the guy running next to you in these pavement sprints. Tyce Carlson (71) and Mark Cassella (96) focus exclusively on the task at hand at Salem in 1995. (Eric Thompson)

to surge around counter-clockwise—it is an absolute no-no on the pavement, where any deviation can spell disaster.

Without the wings pushing down on the tires, it's much easier to slide these non-winged cars. Slippage must be kept to a minimum since it will cause unwanted tire wear and also slow the car. It may also spark an accident.

What is true of engines on short dirt tracks has proven to be true on pavement as well. For example, the Glen Niebel team, which races in USAC, used a V-6 power plant for a number of years with tremendous success. The lighter engine and enhanced ability to apply the power to the track resulted in much up-front running for the team. Less powerful engines are sometimes better suited to non-winged racing, whether on pavement or on dirt.

FROM DIRT TO PAVEMENT AND BACK

In earlier days, when some sanctioning bodies used to run both dirt and pavement tracks, the rule was that the same car had to be used for both track surfaces.

Today, most of the top teams in the few series that run both surfaces have both pavement and dirt cars, but there are still a few teams with less financial support that use a single car for both applications. Unfortunately for them, there is no way a dirt car can be converted to pavement and compete with the pure pavement cars.

Looking at a pavement non-winged sprint car, it's easy to see the differences. As Staab explains, "First, the car sits a lot lower, with the

engine also having a lower position. It's also easy to note that the right side offset is considerably greater with the paved machine. The car is a lot stronger, too, with the front axle having a much larger diameter."

To be sure, the winged and non-winged environments are two different worlds. The drivers who can do both are the best there are.

Opposite: Observe the low stance and right-side offset of these pavement sprint cars at Winchester Speedway in 1995. Some cars carry small front air deflectors, mounted low, for additional downforce. (Phil Kunz)

Top left: Keep that machine as straight as possible and don't make any sudden moves, or you will have big problems. Kevin Thomas is excellent on both counts and can always be found running up front. (Eric Thompson)

Far left: Gus Wassun's pavement sprinter uses a long sweeping hood and a low-mounted air scoop for cooling purposes. The front coil-over shocks are also clearly visible in this greatly offset car. (Phil Kunz)

Near left: Beefy roll cage bars and a face helmet help protect Dave Darland, pictured in 1995, in even the most unforgiving roll. (Eric Thompson)

Great Sprint Drivers— Past and Present

Through the years, the skills of many drivers have shown brightly in sprint cars.

From the 1950s through the 1970s, sprints were an important career-building experience. For many, it was a steppingstone to the big time, the Indianapolis 500 and the Indy car circuit. In the 1990s, drivers are again following this path to the Indy cars. Rich Vogler, for example, with an amazing thirty-five USAC sprint victories, went on to run Indy cars, and recent USAC Sprint Champion Tony Stewart has taken his sprint skills and applied them to the Indy Racing League (IRL) Indy car circuit.

Johnny Rutherford was an active sprint car driver during the 1960s and had eight USAC victories. He was also the USAC sprint champion in 1965. His best-remembered sprint ride took place in 1967, when he left the park at Eldora Speedway and broke both arms in the process. J.R. is a three-time winner at the Brickyard and one of the Indy car circuit's true legends.

Mario Andretti is another member of the old school who used sprint cars to get to the speedway. He was an excellent USAC sprint performer, with nine wins. Mario would also take his skills to NASCAR stock car racing, Indy cars, and Formula One, where he was the world champion.

The king of the sprint-Indy connection is A.J. Foyt, who is possibly the most versatile driver ever to get behind the wheel. He drove everything, and he drove everything well. He won sixty-seven Indy car races, but he also racked up twenty-eight sprint wins, along with checkered flags in just about every other type of racing machine.

Former sprint car driver Gordon Johncock is a two-time Indy winner, and another Gordon, Jeff Gordon, was a tear in both winged and non-winged sprints three decades later. Jeff parlayed these successes into stock car victories, with Winston Cup Championships in 1995 and 1997.

Then too there is the longtime sprint racer of the 1970s and 1980s, the skilled Ken Schrader (who became Jeff Gordon's teammate in the mid-1990s). Schrader was a former USAC sprint champion but was equally adept in any type of open wheel race car.

A lot of fans think of three-time Indy 500 winner Bobby Unser in terms of Indy cars only, but the eldest Unser brother earned his spurs on the dusty sprint car tracks of the Midwest. The same was the case with driver Parnelli Jones, who had his share of success in the sprints. Roger McCluskey was another skilled sprint driver turned Indy car driver. Other sprint greats of the period were Don Branson, Bobby Sweikert, Bobby Vieth, Jud Larsen, Jigs Peters, Eddie Sachs, Elmer George, Rex Easton, Johnny White, Jim McElreath, Greg Weld, and others.

One of the best ever in the sprint cars was Pancho Carter, who won USAC Sprint Championships in 1974 and 1976 and totalled forty-two sprint wins in his career. Tom Sneva is another sprint car graduate who saw some great performances at the Brickyard. The former high school principal was the first ever to turn a 200 MPH lap at Indy. Tom ran the low-slung rear-engine sprinters during the late 1970s, before they were outlawed by USAC.

Opposite: The great USAC Sprint Champion Rollie Beale (40) duels with Jim Malloy at New Breman (Ohio) Speedway in 1969. (Ken Coles)

This page, clockwise from top left: Tony Stewart; Ken Schrader at Eldora Speedway in 1981; Jan Opperman at Eldora in 1974; A.J. Foyt, photographed minutes before winning his first major dirt race in 1960 at DuQuion, Illinois; and Mario Andretti in 1974. (Photos by John Mahoney and Ken Coles)

Opposite: Superstar sprint car and Indy car driver Pancho Carter at speed in one of Steve Stapp's cars at Terre Haute in 1976. (Ken Coles)

Opposite: Larry Dickson and Gary Bettenhausen always put on a good show; here they are in a 1969 showdown. Their battles came to be known as the "Gary and Larry Show." (Ken Coles)

Top, left to right: Sheldon Kinser, at Kokomo in 1981; Jac Haudenschild in 1995; and Steve Kinser at Bloomington in 1994. (Photos by John Mahoney and Randy Jones)

Left: Rich Vogler is all concentration as he waits for a race early in his illustrious career. (David Tucker)

It also goes without saying that Gary Bettenhausen has a sprint connection, being one of the best in the machines. Gary won the USAC sprint titles in both 1969 and 1971 and finished second in 1968 and 1970, during four spirited years of competition with Larry Dickson. Other drivers during that same time period were Sammy Sessions, Billy Cassella, Larry Rice, Lee Kunzman, Tom Bigelow, and Rollie Beale. Rollie Beale was a USAC sprint champion and later the USAC sprint supervisor.

Second-generation driver John Andretti used the sprints, where he proved very talented, to get to the Indy cars, and, eventually, to a full-time NASCAR Winston Cup ride.

Looking back in time to the so-called outlaws of the 1960s and 1970s, a number of drivers' names come into focus. Probably the most famous was the irrepressible Jan Opperman, known for his floppy cowboy hat, long hair, and unbelievable skills on the track. He was able to make it to Indy, but he had to cut his hair before it happened!

Other drivers during those early winged-sprint days included legends Rick Ferkel, Kenny Weld, and Bobby Allen. Bobby Allen's career extended into the 1990s, including a win at the famous King's Royal race at Eldora Speedway.

During the 1970s and 1980s, the West Coast exploits of Bubby Jones and Dean Thompson secured many wins and championships between them.

Of course, through the Big Car days earlier this century there were numerous great names, many of which have vanished from memo-ry as the decades slide by. Days of victory and glory at dusty fair-ground tracks—many drivers raced just about every night of the week at a different track—laid the foundation for sprint car racing today. One star of these early days was Tommy Hinnershitz, who won a tremendous number of races.

During the 1980s, the performance of Doug Wolfgang set the standard for sprint car excellence. Unfortunately, a serious accident in the early 1990s slowed his illustrious career. And one of the sport's most popular sprint drivers ever is Brad Doty, who was seriously injured in an accident in 1988, at the apex of his career. He remains active in the sport on TV and through charitable efforts.

Without a doubt, the stars of the World of Outlaws organization are today's sprint superstars. The shining star of that organization, in turn, is the incomparable Steve Kinser. Kinser has hundreds of sprint victories and many World of Outlaw titles.

In fact, many Kinsers have excelled in sprints, including Steve's dad, Bobby, who still raced in the mid-1990s. Other members of the Kinser clan include three-time USAC Sprint Champion Sheldon; his son, Sheldon, Jr.; and outstanding runners Mark, Kelly, and Randy. Many sets of brothers race in sprints, and it has been that way throughout the sport's history.

There are other stars in the modern group, including second-generation driver Dave Blaney, who won the World of Outlaw title in 1995, and longtime competitor Jac Haudenschild. Other 1990s stars competing in the World of Outlaws series are Andy Hillenburg, Danny Lasoski, Stevie Smith, Sammy Swindell, Johnny Herrera,

Top, left to right: Danny Smith in 1994; Stevie Smith; Joey Saldana; and Jac Haudenschild. (Photos by Randy Jones, Bill Holder, and Larry Reese)

Left: Four-time All Star Champion Frankie Kerr, shown at Eldora in 1995, comes from the old school. He does the majority of the work on his cars himself. If something goes wrong mechanically, he will tell you that there is nobody to blame but himself. (Eric Thompson)

Top, near right: Jeff Gordon started driving sprint cars when he was only thirteen. By age twenty-four, he was the NASCAR Winston Cup champion. (Gary McKisson)

Top, far right: The late Robbie Stanley, pictured in 1993 at Eldora, was Mr. Versatility, winning one All Star winged sprint car title and three USAC non-winged championships. He died while racing a sprinter in the early 1990s. (John Mahoney)

Bottom right: All Star Champion Fred Linder was a quiet guy out of his car, but on the track he spoke loudly. Always the man to beat, he was well known with his #3X cars. (David Tucker)

Opposite, top: Dave Blaney shows the effects of fatigue from the brutal ten-month World of Outlaws schedule. He was the series champion in 1996 and moved to stock cars in 1998. (Eric Thompson)

Opposite, bottom: These piercing eyes belong to the man many consider the best sprint car driver ever— Steve Kinser. (Eric Thompson)

Below: Johnny Herrera's aggressive style on the track has made him a favorite of the fans. (Larry Reese)

Joey Saldana (dad Joe Saldana also starred with USAC), Randy Hannigan, and more.

Current All Star organization stars include Frankie Kerr; Kevin Huntley; brothers Kenny and Dean Jacobs; Joey Saldana; Texan Gary Wright; Pennsylvania runners Lance Dewease, Freddy Rahmer, and Keith Kauffman; California driver Brent Keating; Hoosier Danny Smith; and longtime Tennessee runner Bobby Davis, Jr. Many others are also successful in the sprints. There are even Limited Sprint drivers who are starting to become household names, such as standout Gary Lee Maier, a Missouri native.

Jack Hewitt is known for his ability to succeed in many kinds of race cars. This versatile competitor from Ohio can drive anything, including non-winged sprint cars on dirt with USAC and winged sprint cars (in which he has won fifty-six All Star races), as well as winged and non-winged cars on pavement.

Many other great drivers have made history in sprint cars—too many to mention. The guys who drive the powerful sprint cars are something special and as central to the sport as the cars they drive. Profiles of some of the most exceptional are on the pages that follow.

Phil Kunz

STEVE KINSER
born June 2, 1955
Bloomington, Indiana

He is the king of sprint car racing in the U.S., there is no doubt. Steve Kinser has been at the top of the sport for many years, with many championships in the World of Outlaws series. In addition, he has been a winner in the biggest special shows, such as the Kings Royal race and the Knoxville Nationals.

His win total with the World of Outlaws is about four hundred, an amazing number when you consider the intense competition of the series, with roughly a dozen drivers capable of winning every time out. His best year was 1987, when he won an unbelievable fifty-six races.

Steve is now over forty years old, and he has been in sprint cars for about half of those years. By today's standards, however, he was an "old" twenty-one when he started driving those powerful winged racers.

"They didn't let the real young guys drive these cars back when I started," he explains.

Steve says he thinks he is just as good a driver as he was ten years ago, maybe better. "One thing for sure, I know I'm a lot smarter after driving for all these years."

As any sprint car fan will tell you, much of Steve's success has been directly related to his first cousin and longtime crew chief, Karl Kinser. The two could think as one and were tremendously effective. They parted company in the mid-1990s, with Karl taking over as crew chief for his son Mark. That Kinser pair went on to the 1996 World of Outlaws championship.

Racing is definitely in the Kinser genes; a number of other family members are also involved with sprint car racing. Steve's brother Randy runs effectively on the short tracks in Ohio and Indiana, and cousin Kelly has been a longtime performer with the All Star Circuit of Champions.

Steve says that huge improvements have been made to the sprinters during the course of his illustrious career. "I think the tires and engines have seen the greatest improvements."

To drive these cars, you have to be in top shape. To that end, Steve trains hard in the off-season, playing racquetball and running. A two-time state wrestling champion in high school, Steve has the strength necessary to manhandle his car to victory.

Steve Kinser used his driving skills in stock car racing as well. In 1995, Kenny Bernstein gave Steve a chance to drive his Winston Cup stock car. Unfortunately, for a number of reasons, it was not a successful venture. Steve did show, however, that with competition equipment, he could compete at a high level. He won one of the International Race of Champions (IROC) races.

Steve's longtime dream of running at Indianapolis was answered by the IRL Indy Car league, which enabled Steve to run at the Brickyard in 1997. He performed well, and there could be more IRL running in the future for Steve. Time will tell.

But until something else comes along, it will continue to be sprint car racing. Steve Kinser is the king of the winged sprint car sport, and there is no indication that his reign will end anytime soon.

Gilmore-Foyt photo

A.J. FOYT
born January 16, 1935
Houston, Texas

One tough Texan. That's the perception many have of A.J. Foyt, the result of his personal demeanor and his aggressive style on the racetrack.

Like others of his era, A.J. drove just about any type of car, sprint cars included. In part because he understood the mechanical workings of so many cars, it didn't seem to matter what A.J. was wheeling. One of the best in the sprints, he is probably even better known for his successes at the Indianapolis Motor Speedway, where he won the Indy 500 three times and came close to the checkered on a number of other occasions.

The burning desire for success that drove A.J.'s remarkable career was there when he was racing the USAC Sprints. In 1957, he appeared for the first

time in the eleventh position but had no wins. A year later, he had moved up to second in this super-tough series, finishing just behind Indy legend Eddie Sachs.

A.J. was second again in the nation's premier sprint series in 1959, behind only Don Branson. There was a pair of wins that year; at Salem, Indiana, and at his hometown Houston track. In 1960, A.J. ran with the leaders again, finishing third behind Parnelli Jones and Branson. There were three wins that season.

A.J. kept running the sprints well into the 1960s with third, fourth, second, and fourth place finishes. After 1964, he started concentrating on the Indy Cars.

Now a team owner in the IRL Indy Car series, A.J. Foyt will forever be remembered for his tenacity on and off the track. Whether in a sprint car on some dusty bull ring or on the two and one-half mile ribbon of Daytona or Indianapolis, he did everything he could to win. Finishing second was never enough.

John Mahoney

RICH VOGLER

(deceased)
born July 26, 1950
Glen Ellyn, Illinois

Rich Vogler was driven—whatever it took to win, this sprint car driver did. If there was a race to be won, he did everything he could to get the job done. Everything.

That's the way he lived and the way he died. Rich Vogler was killed in a sprint car at Salem Speedway, while he was running well in front of the field—as he would have liked it if it had to happen. The freak accident halted an amazing career that started in the early 1970s.

Every time Rich stepped into a car, be it a sprint car, midget, championship dirt car, or Indy car, he was definitely in contention for the win. His entire heart and soul concentrated on the task at hand. He knew the mechanics of each car and

what it took to make it go fast. He arrived at the track and did much of the work on the car himself, setting it up to his liking.

"I really don't think you can be a good sprint car driver unless you understand how the car works. I also have this theory that there is a fastest groove around the track, and I'll keep looking until I find it," he once said. Rich Vogler usually found that fine line.

Just how successful was he? He won an amazing ninety-five midget and thirty-five sprint races. He won the USAC Sprint Championship twice and was second three times.

The son of a former driver, Don Vogler, Rich Vogler came by his open wheel racing skills naturally. "My dad never drove anything with fenders and was one of the nation's best midget drivers during the late 1960s and early 1970s. He finished in the top ten in the USAC midget points a number of times." Tragically, Don Vogler was killed on the track in a midget race.

Had it not been for his unfortunate and entirely too early death, Rich Vogler would undoubtedly have used his sprint and midget experience to jump to bigger national race activities. He had tried Indy cars

a number of times with under-powered cars and proved that he could make them go as fast as they were capable of running. He also attempted stock car racing with NASCAR.

After his death, his mother, Eleanor, established a scholarship fund in Rich's name. The program has helped provide a number of children of racing families with a college education.

Rich Vogler was one of the most versatile drivers in history, capable of taking any type of open wheel car to the front of the pack. Had his life not been cut short at the peak of his career, there could have been much more to tell of his story.

Bill Holder

GARY BETTENHAUSEN

born November 18, 1941
Monrovia, Indiana

Bettenhausen is a name that rides in the annals of open wheel racing through the years. It all started for the Bettenhausen family with Tony, who was considered one of the best ever to wheel the speedy Indy cars at the Brickyard.

Tony's family included three sons who also loved racing, and they all gave it a shot. Tony, Jr. drove both the sprints and Indy cars, but ended his career to become a team manager, a position he retains in the late 1990s. The youngest son, Merle, ran the sprints but had a serious accident that cost him an arm.

Then there is the oldest son, Gary. Gary's long career has included racing stock cars and Indy cars, but his greatest recognition probably comes from his long and super suc-

cessful sprint car career with the United States Auto Club.

Gary's name first appeared on USAC position charts in 1967 in forty-third position, but he moved up quickly. In 1968, he roared up to second position, just behind Larry Dickson; the resulting dual lasted for a number of years and received a lot of national publicity.

In 1970, Gary got revenge and won the title by a huge margin (779 to 590 points). Dickson came back strong in 1971, edging Gary out for the championship. But, like a bouncing ball, Gary came back strong in 1972, with a close win over Dickson. Bettenhausen continued to run through the 1970s on a more limited basis, his focus increasingly on other forms of racing. However, he didn't lose the touch and finished fifth in the USAC points in 1980.

Gary's career was set back in the 1980s, when he suffered a serious arm injury in an open wheel accident. Still, he soldiered on and continued to run on occasion in the 1990s.

John Mahoney

PANCHO CARTER
born June 11, 1950
Brownstown, Indiana

He was the son of famous Indy driver Duane Carter—in fact, he was Duane Carter, Jr., but everybody called him by the nickname he picked up as a kid.

He was an excellent Indy car driver and sat on the pole at the 1985 Indy 500 in an American-built Buick V-6 power plant. But most people recall Pancho Carter as one of the best non-winged sprint car drivers in history. Most of his racing was done with the United States Auto Club.

His name first appeared in the USAC sprint standings in 1971, when he finished thirtieth in the points. In 1973, he was up to sixth and on a roll. The following year, he took his first title with seven wins. He

was fourth in 1975 but came back in 1976 to capture another title. There were a dozen victories that sparkling season, with one stretch of four wins coming in a row.

He finished third in 1977, even though he missed fourteen sprint races, as other types of racing were starting to catch his attention. Still, he won seven races. In all, he won forty-two USAC sprint races against competition that was as tough as it gets. It didn't seem to make much difference whether Pancho was racing on pavement or dirt; he was equally effective on both. He was also adept in the midgets, where he had twenty-three career victories.

His tremendous success aside, the thing that many fans remember about Pancho's racing days is the openness and friendliness that made him such a favorite.

Pancho's brother Dana also wheeled the sprints and midgets and won a number of races before his life was cut tragically short by a heart attack.

With a name like Carter, it's probably no surprise that Pancho's two sons are both driving learning-level cars.

Jerry Clum

JACK HEWITT
born July 8, 1951
Troy, Ohio

He is a folk hero to his many fans in the Midwest. If you were ever to cast a sprint car driver as a gunslinger in a western movie, Jack Hewitt would have to be your man.

It seems like Jack, now in his late forties, has been around forever, and his career shows no signs of slowing. No one recommends asking Jack himself when he will bow out.

During his early days, Jack was a bit of an outlaw, sporting a full beard. The tough attitude remains, and he has never been one to step away from confrontation if he thinks the cause is just. Jack has a burning desire to win. The record shows that his desire plus his incredible talent have paid big dividends.

This is a driver from the old school, equally at home in either an open wheel or stock car. But through the years, he has probably been best in the sprint cars, where he is second on the total wins list for the All Star sanctioning body. He also has some forty USAC sprint wins. He has won championships with both organizations.

It does not seem to make any difference what type of sprint car Jack drives, whether it has a wing or not, or whether he drives on pavement or dirt. Give Jack a couple laps to get accustomed to the car and, most likely, he'll be running up front very quickly.

Jack is the "middle man" in a racing family. His father, Don, who died in an industrial accident in 1997, was an outstanding sprint driver who had many wins. Don could always be seen supporting Jack whenever he was on the track. Then there is Jack's son Cody, definitely a chip off the old block, who has shown real talent in kart racing.

In the early 1990s, Jack experienced one of the low points of his distinguished career when he was involved in a serious accident at Eldora Speedway. A sprint car he was passing lost control and came down on top of his car. Jack suffered a seri-

ous head injury but, amid ominous reports, surprised doctors with his quick recovery. Within months, he was back on the track. It takes a lot to keep this guy down.

Some day, Jack Hewitt will retire, and it just won't seem the same when his sprinter is not out there running for the front. He's definitely one of the sprint car legends!

IMS Properties

MARIO ANDRETTI
born February 28, 1940
Nazareth, Pennsylvania

Mario Andretti is truly an American icon. When you hear somebody say, "Who does he think he is, Mario Andretti?" as a car races by on the freeway, you get an idea of just how legendary this man is.

Much of Mario's renown probably comes from the wide range of racing in which he has participated throughout the years. It must be recalled that his career began on dusty dirt tracks in non-winged sprint cars, many times running with the United States Auto Club. It was a tough deal because he was out there learning his trade with the best sprint drivers in the country. Drivers like Bobby Unser, Parnelli Jones, Johnny Rutherford, and many others challenged Mario early in his career. Those days in sprint cars played an important part in starting this lengthy and great career.

Of course, Mario's greatest acclaim has come from his huge success in the open wheel Indy cars, including a 1969 victory at Indianapolis. In all, there were thirty-three wins in the championship cars and two Indy car titles.

During the 1960s, the sprints were one of the best ways to get to Indy, and that's exactly the route that Mario utilized. With his Indy car success, Mario moved to the international Formula One circuit, where he won the World Championship in 1977.

There was more. On occasion he took time to run a NASCAR stock car. It is not surprising that he did well in that venue, too, and was a one-time winner of the Daytona 500 early in his career.

Now retired, Mario is still a spokesman for the sport and is heavily involved in the Indy car career of his son Michael, who is one of the top drivers in the Championship Auto Racing Teams (CART) Indy car circuit.

Many will tell you that Mario Andretti would have to be on the short list of the best drivers ever. And remember, it all started for this superstar with the sprint cars!

Ken Coles

ROGER McCLUSKEY
(deceased)
born August 30, 1930
Indianapolis, Indiana

Roger McCluskey lived life to the hilt. During the 1960s and 1970s, he was on top of the racing world, driving a montage of racing machines.

A racer's racer, Roger was long looked up to by other drivers. Early in his career his cohorts elected him their representative on the USAC board of directors. Then, following his competition days, he served as USAC's director of competition. His management skills were excellent.

His was also a racing career that few exceeded. Roger drove just about everything, including Indy cars, sprint cars, midgets, stock cars, supermodifieds, and even international road race cars, and he excelled in everything he drove.

During his career, Roger won USAC National Championships in three different divisions, twice in two of the divisions. The sprint car titles came in 1963 and 1966, the stock car championships in 1969 and 1970, and the Indy car crown in 1973. His total wins are equally impressive, with twenty-three in sprints, an identical number in stock cars, and five in the Indy cars.

Racing began for Roger at the age of seventeen, when he participated in a jalopy race in Phoenix, Arizona. His sprint car career began in the late 1950s. One of the first cars he drove was owned by the daughter of Tony Hulman, the owner of the Indianapolis Motor Speedway.

Roger's first good year in the sprint cars came in 1962, when he finished a close second to Parnelli Jones. Then, in his first championship season, in 1963, Roger ran like gangbusters, completely blowing away the competition. He had 814 winning points compared to the runner-up's total of 505. The second USAC sprint title, three years later, also came in a dominating style, with a 194-point victory over Mario Andretti. There were nine wins that season.

Roger had a number of nasty injuries in his impressive career, probably the worst of which came in sprint cars. It happened in 1964 at the Reading (Pennsylvania) Fairgrounds, when his car took a number of vicious midair rolls and then whirled through a series of end-over-end flips, finally halting upside-down in mid-track. Roger suffered a badly mangled arm in the crash.

One of Roger's career goals was to win the Indy 500. He ran at the Brickyard eighteen times; his best effort was a third place finish in 1973, the same year he won the Indy car title.

His son, Roger, Jr., has acquired the open wheel racing bug from his dad and is an outstanding midget driver.

A class act, that would be the best way to describe Roger McCluskey. And in this success story, too, sprint cars played a big role.

Ken Coles

BOBBY UNSER
born February 20, 1938
Albuquerque, New Mexico

Mention the name Unser in open wheel circles and you'll definitely get raised eyebrows. Besides Bobby, there is legendary brother Al, with four Indy 500 victories. And there's also Al's son, Al, Jr., a star driver for the Roger Penske team on the CART Indy car circuit.

Bobby is the dean of the racing family, and, with his three Indy victories, is considered one of the top Indy car pilots of all time. Like many others, he earned his spurs with early sprint car racing in USAC. Running a sprint car in the 1960s and 1970s was a solid ticket to Indy, though that is no longer the case.

Bobby recalls his 1960s USAC sprint car racing with great fondness. "It was a lot different

in those days. First of all, we were driving without any power steering. I can remember driving on some of the fast high-banked tracks right up against the wall and having bloody hands after the race was over. Then too, we were also running with skinny tires, compared to the wide ones that today's sprint cars use. Even so, it was great fun out there running against the likes of Johnny Rutherford, A.J. Foyt, Don Branson, Mario [Andretti], and others."

Bobby first appeared in the USAC sprint season points in 1963, finishing only thirty-fifth. Things got better in a hurry. A year later, he was eleventh and won his first race, at Gardena, California. In 1965, Bobby was third, behind Johnny Rutherford and Greg Weld. He had a trio of consecutive wins that season at Fort Wayne, Indiana; Reading, Pennsylvania; and Salem, Indiana. He was third again in 1966, following Roger McCluskey and Mario Andretti. His final year of sprints came in 1967, when he ran only eleven of twenty-seven races but still finished an impressive thirteenth in the points.

Today, Bobby continues to be in the limelight as a national TV commentator for Indy car racing events.

John Mahoney

STEVE BUTLER
born September 26, 1956
Kokomo, Indiana

Think about the powerful non-winged sprint cars that run with the United States Auto Club. Some stars no longer on the circuit have remained in the memories of the fans, and Steve Butler— now retired—was one of the brightest of these.

Steve was particularly tough— smooth as silk!—driving a sprint car on pavement. But he was equally talented on the dirt, with a giant wing over his head. He had to be good in both realms because when he ran with the USAC series, both types of sprint cars competed.

This talented sprint car driver proved that he could do both by winning the USAC Sprint Championship in 1986, 1987, and 1988. In all, he had twenty-five sprint car wins against

very tough competition. His last sprint championship year, he doubled up and also won the USAC Championship Dirt Car title, a series that runs both pavement and dirt tracks.

Driving a sprint car on dirt and pavement are very different, as Steve will tell you. "You have to be very smooth with the car on pavement and try to save the tires, which are taking more of a beating than on dirt," he explains.

"On the dirt, it's entirely different. The track is constantly changing and you have to change your driving style with it. After driving mostly pavement, it sometimes takes a little while to get used to the dirt again."

He says that he learned a lot from driving go-karts and quarter midgets during his younger days. "I learned to have a positive attitude and concentrate while I'm driving. The kart racing also taught me to get over a tough loss and to be able to put it behind me. Racing is a lot like life, with its ups and downs, and you've got to take your lumps and move on."

Interestingly, this bespectacled, ever-smiling guy didn't come directly from karts to sprints.

There were five wild and crazy years driving motorcycles before he got into racing machines with four wheels.

Steve would have loved to have raced at Indianapolis, but it just didn't work out for him. There was a try in 1989, "but I crashed hard and didn't make the big show."

Unlike many of the other top sprint car drivers, Steve held down a full-time job during his entire racing career. One has to wonder how well he might have done had he been able to focus his attention completely on racing.

One of the nicest drivers in racing, Steve Butler went about his business quietly and well. The only noise normally associated with his work was the cheering of the crowd as he took yet another checkered flag.

Tom de Vette

ROBBIE STANLEY

(deceased)
born November 16, 1967
Concord, North Carolina

Robbie Stanley was good, really good in the sprint cars, any kind of sprint car, on either dirt or pavement, with wings or without.

Robbie's versatility helped him win championships with two different sanctioning bodies. In 1989, he won the All Star Circuit of Champions series that races winged sprint cars. Then, he made a move to the mostly pavement USAC series with non-winged sprinters. He adapted quickly to the new type of racing and won three straight USAC titles, from 1990–1992.

Following this accomplishment, his thoughts turned to Busch Grand National stock cars, where he had shown promise. But there were still sprint car races now and then. A sprint car accident in 1994

took his life at the high-banked Winchester Speedway. His car spun in the fourth turn and was struck by another, ultimately erupting into flames.

Had Robbie survived the crash, it is unlikely that he would have blamed anybody for the accident. He was known to say that an accident "was just one of those racing deals." That's the way he was.

In retrospect, Robbie's success with the pavement sprint cars should have been expected. He started his career in the seat of a quarter midget and competed at the national level. It certainly didn't hurt that Robbie helped his dad, Ron, build quarter midgets; The younger Stanley assisted and learned a lot about open wheel cars in the process.

Robbie ran on the edge, that's for sure, but he was also a student of the sport and was constantly thinking about it. He was able to transfer easily from dirt to pavement without any apparent decrease in capability.

"You have to keep your sprinter as straight as possible on the pavement. It's not like the dirt, where you can use the power of the engine to get out of trouble. You have to use

the steering wheel more on the pavement," Robbie explained.

Not many knew it, but Robbie did his open wheel driving with a knee that was badly injured in high school. Driving was extremely painful, and he knew that he would have to have a knee replacement some day. "I'll race 'til I have to have the operation, and then I'll race afterward," he vowed.

Just before his death, Robbie said, "I want to master each type of racing before I move on to the next step."

He certainly mastered sprint cars, and he'll be remembered as one of the best ever in the powerful open wheel cars.

Rest well, Robbie Stanley. You are not forgotten.

NASCAR photo

KEN SCHRADER

born May 29, 1955
Fenton, Missouri

Although NASCAR regular Ken Schrader has been driving Winston Cup stock cars for several years, many in his multitude of fans still think of him as a short track open wheel driver.

That's where it all started for Ken, and short track racing is something that he hasn't let go of through his stock car years. Ken Schrader is a one-of-a-kind driver. When there is an open NASCAR date, you can find him at some short track driving a sprint, midget, modified, stock car, whatever.

Admittedly, his activity has slowed somewhat in recent years, but he still comes back to the short track on occasion. The connection is strong.

Ken started in stock cars in the late 1970s, taking the USAC Stock Car Championship. He could have concentrated on that venue, but he also liked other types of race cars. To that end, he tried the open wheel Silver Crown cars and won that title in 1982. The following year, he took the sprint cars seriously and won the USAC title in that division, too.

During the 1980s, there were periods when Kenny would go absolutely nuts and run a ton of races in a short period of time. That usually happened during the month of May, when there were gobs of open wheel races being run around the Indianapolis area. If Ken could make any or all of those races, he was there.

Speaking of Indianapolis, this good-natured driver gave Indy cars a try in 1983. The attempt was unsuccessful and started him thinking about stock cars. After all, he had run USAC stock cars and also a number of stock cars on dirt and paved short tracks.

In 1984, Ken got his first chance at Winston Cup racing and liked the whole scene. A year later, he got serious and was named the NASCAR rookie of the year. He has run up front ever since and is always considered a threat to win.

Needless to say, the heavy stock cars were quite a change from the sprinters. "The stock cars are a lot heavier and are less responsive. It took a little getting used to, but it's still racing, and I've enjoyed my career with NASCAR."

During the mid-1990s, Kenny was a member of the strongest team in Winston Cup racing, the Hendrick Racing Team. It was like old home week, because one of his teammates was another former open wheeler of note, Jeff Gordon.

It just goes to show that the sprint cars are an excellent learning ground, as Ken Schrader has proven in convincing fashion.

Randy Jones

JEFF GORDON
born August 4, 1971
Pittsboro, Indiana

It's an amazing story, right out of the American dream. It happened to Jeff Gordon, who used open wheel racing to vault himself into the big time of Winston Cup racing, which he has dominated in the 1990s.

His open wheel career was as amazing as his later stock car career has been. Jeff started out with quarter midgets and karts, where he won at the national level and was a national champion in the quarter midgets several times.

Jeff started driving winged sprint cars when he was only thirteen years old. In that first sprint car season, in 1985, he ran with the All Star sprints. That season, he was the third quickest qualifier several times

and finished just out of the top ten a number of times. Jeff ran on many tracks and did not have a home track advantage, which made his accomplishments even more impressive.

After being barred from a number of tracks because of his young age, Jeff got going strong in the late 1980s and ran well with USAC, the All Stars, and the World of Outlaws. In this flurry of activity, he also added the USAC Silver Crown cars to his schedule and scored well there, too.

Nineteen ninety was a great year for the polished young driver, as he won eight USAC national midget features, three in the Western States series, and took the USAC midget title.

The sprint cars and midgets are no longer the way to get to the Indy cars, but had Jeff Gordon chosen to go that way, he undoubtedly could have made it. But the Indy Cars were not in Jeff's plans. He felt that the stock cars were the best route, and he moved into Busch Grand National competition in 1991.

At the time, he indicated that the transition from the light, speedy sprint cars to the heavy stockers was a big one.

"But I was doing a lot of open wheel racing on pavement, and that really helped my move to the stock cars," Jeff explains.

It was not long before Jeff got the feel of the stock cars. In 1995, he was named Winston Cup rookie of the year and won the Winston Cup title. In 1996, he won ten races, but was beaten out for the title by teammate Terry Labonte. In 1997, he got it back together and beat Mark Martin and Dale Jarrett to win the title.

Recently, Jeff had an opportunity to view one of his old sprint cars that had been restored. He was extremely excited when he saw it. "I can't believe that I used to race these cars. It was one of the greatest times of my life when I was running the short dirt tracks in the Midwest. I was just a teenager and having a ball."

Without a doubt, with his Winston Cup success, Jeff Gordon continues to have a ball, these days in the stock cars!

Bill Holder

JAN OPPERMAN
(deceased)
born February 9, 1939
Noxon, Montana

In the early days of sprint car racing, a single driver was designated "the outlaw." It was a hard-won title.

The late Jan Opperman (who died in 1997) personified the name. He was not attached to any particular organization and ran wherever the money was. His style was another "outlaw" characteristic—flat out!

Jan looked the part; the long hair cascading over his shoulders was far from the clean-cut look of many of his competitors. His car usually carried a large cross denoting his love of religion.

Jan drove with just about every sanctioning body and impressed them all. He was one of the early stars of the All

Stars organization in the early 1970s and won a number of the organization's brutal one hundred–lap races.

He would later run again with the All Stars and with the World of Outlaws, bringing along a horde of fans wherever he competed.

On one occasion, Jan was given a chance at the ultimate experience for an open wheel driver—running at the Indianapolis Motor Speedway. There was one outlaw characteristic that had to be changed for the experience: He had to cut his hair, which he begrudgingly did. The Indy attempt did not work out, so it was back to the sprint cars that he loved.

Sprint cars would eventually take his life. First, he was in a crash that caused serious injuries. His family urged him to retire, but that was not Jan's style. He came back and unfortunately was involved in another crash, which caused a serious head injury.

After the second accident, Jan's family had to provide him with full-time care until his death in 1997. It was a sad ending to a no-holds-barred career.

The death of Jan Opperman brings to light the danger of sprint cars, with their incredible power and precarious performance. But it was the life that Jan wanted to live, and he lived it to the hilt.

WoO photo

DAVE BLANEY
born October 24, 1962
Cortland, Ohio

The Blaneys are an open wheel racing family. First, there is dad, who is recognized as one of the best modified racers ever.

Dad passed the racing bug on to his sons Dale and Dave, who have both responded. Following an excellent college basketball career, along with a shot at the pros, Dale came back to sprint cars and was the All Star Circuit of Champions title winner in both 1995 and 1996.

Dave, who was also a talented basketball player in high school, went directly into racing after graduation. He actually started his career in go-karts before jumping into the powerful sprint cars. He has been in the sprints ever since, usually running about a hundred races a year with the top gun World of Outlaws organization, where he has become one of the nation's most popular drivers.

It's a tough life, with late hours, a demanding travel schedule, and a lot of hard work. "But I've learned to get used to it," he explains. "I've learned to relax and can sleep just about anywhere."

Much of Dave's fantastic career was run for owner Casey Luna, the former lieutenant governor of New Mexico, in a rare Ford-powered machine. It was with this team that he won the prestigious King's Royal race at Eldora Speedway. He was also the 1995 World of Outlaws champion. Through the years, he has always finished high in sprint car racing's toughest series. He does not have a preference for a particular type of track. "Doesn't matter," he says. "As long as the car is set up right, I like them all. To succeed in the sprint cars, you have to work closely with your mechanic and crew and end up thinking as one."

In his many years of sprint car racing, Dave feels that the biggest improvements have come in the power plants. "The engines are making about 150 more horsepower than they were when I first started. It's usually all the power I can use on the track."

Dave has also driven the wingless USAC Silver Crown cars, and, not surprisingly, has run up front much of the time. He has also driven an Automobile Race Car Association (ARCA) stock car on a number of occasions and has shown surprising success in the heavy race cars with very little experience.

Whether he will move on to other realms of racing and leave sprint cars remains to be seen. Whatever he does, Dave will be long remembered as one of the very best sprint car drivers of the 1990s.

The Crown Jewels— Famous Tracks and Races

Almost synonymous with sprint cars are the places and big events where they run. Venues like Eldora, Knoxville, William's Grove, Ascot, and Silver Dollar are a few of the past and present ovals that have seen the greats of the sport reach their glory. Then there are the great sprint races that through the years have continued to draw fans by the thousands; the King's Royal, Knoxville Nationals, Gold Cup, Historical Big One, and other names easily fall off the tongues of true sprint car fans. Here's a closer look at the Crown Jewel races and the tracks on which they are run:

ELDORA (OHIO) SPEEDWAY

Almost as famous as the track itself is its owner, Earl Baltes, who has been one of the sport's most popular individuals for many years. He has entertained sprints since USAC first started running at his track, in the early 1960s, along with all of its famous stars.

In 1982, Baltes initiated the famous King's Royal event, which through the years has paid the winner a princely sum of $50,000. All of the top guns from across the U.S. converge on this super fast, high-banked facility, and the action is furious. Steve Kinser (three times), Doug Wolfgang, and Dave Blaney are all previous winners of the event.

Baltes initiated a second event in 1993, called the Historical Big One—and big it is, with $100,000 going to the first driver under the checkered flag.

In the 1970s, Eldora held multiday shows called the Eldora Nationals, which brought in big crowds of cars and fans. The track has also been a part of the All Star Sprint Speedweek, a seven-day series of races at seven tracks across the Buckeye State. The popularity of the series has caused the concept to be copied in Indiana and Pennsylvania.

The final gem at Eldora is the long-standing USAC Four-Crown Nationals, which has midgets, championship dirt cars, and stock cars on its agenda, in addition to non-winged sprints.

KNOXVILLE (IOWA) SPEEDWAY

Right there at the top of the biggest sprint events is the annual undertaking at Knoxville Speedway. It's called the Knoxville Nationals, and the four-day event attracts huge crowds. Several hundred cars and drivers are usually on hand to contend with the best in the nation for big money. In recent years, the event has been carried live on national TV.

The Knoxville Nationals began in 1961, with the early races competing non-winged sprints. Many of the great drivers have run and won the nationals. Not surprisingly, the last five in a row have been won by the King of the Outlaws, Steve Kinser. Through the 1995 season, Steve had won the event eleven times. Other multiple winners include Kenny Weld (four), Taylor Weld (three), and Doug Wolfgang (three). The track also houses the Sprint Car Hall of Fame.

WILLIAM'S GROVE (PENNSYLVANIA) SPEEDWAY

The big event at this Pennsylvania track is called the National

Opposite: During the 1960s, some of the biggest sprint car races in the nation were held at Eldora Speedway in western Ohio. In this amazing photo from 1962, Johnny Rutherford (63), Roger McCluskey (5), and Parnelli Jones (1) duel for the lead. (Ken Coles)

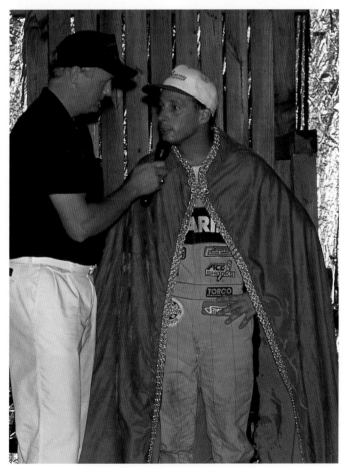

Open, which has been run since 1963. Many familiar names crop up among past winners, including, recently, the Kinser clan (Steve and Mark). Multiple winners through the years include Bobby Adamson, with two wins; Kenny Weld, with three victories; Steve Kinser, with a trio; and Stevie Smith, with two wins. Interestingly, Stevie's father, Steve Smith, won the event in 1981.

ANDERSON (INDIANA) SPEEDWAY
Many fans will tell you that the Little 500 is the most famous of all the sprint car classics. It's certainly the longest running—it started in 1949. It's run on pavement with non-winged cars on a tiny quarter-mile oval with an amazing thirty-three cars starting Indy 500–style in eleven rows—perhaps a tribute to the big race at the Brickyard, which runs the very next day, Memorial Day.

Driver Bob Frey has been a dominant force in this race in recent years; he's had five wins, four coming in a row. He also finished second twice.

The event is characterized by the many types of sprinters that run in it; some of the cars are decades old, some are brand new, and all come in different styles.

SKAGIT (WASHINGTON) SPEEDWAY
Skagit Speedway is best known for the Super Dirt Cup, although there actually have been a number of different Dirt Cups through the years. From 1972 through 1976, the event was called the Northwest Dirt Cup, and it was run at three different Washington tracks: Sky Valley, Skagit, and Elma Speedways. In 1977 the event was

Opposite: This ground-pounding action is typical of Eldora's two big events: the King's Royal and the Historical Big One, both of which attract the top sprint car teams in the nation. (Phil Kunz)

Top, far left: The man behind the King's Royal and Historical Big One is the charismatic Earl Baltes, who does what it takes to keep sprint car fans coming back for more. (John Mahoney)

Top, near left: Andy Hillenburg accepts the accolades for winning the 1995 Gold Cup from Silver Dollar Speedway promoter John Padjen. (Donna Peter)

Left: Dave Blaney, long a World of Outlaws front-runner, is shown in the traditional winner's robe at the 1995 King's Royal event at Eldora Speedway. (Eric Thompson)

Right: Steve Kinser's grin reflects winnings of $100,000 at the 1995 Historical Big One at Eldora Speedway. (Eric Thompson)

Opposite: Frank Riddle (88) battles eventual winner Jeff Bloom at the 1991 Little 500 at Anderson Speedway. (Randy Jones)

moved exclusively to Skagit Speedway, where it was called the Skagit Super Dirt Cup. In 1984, it was renamed the Jim Raper Memorial Super Dirt Cup, and it retains that name to this day.

The predominant personality in this race by far has been Jimmy Sills, who has won the title half a dozen times. Tim Green has won the event three times.

SILVER DOLLAR (CALIFORNIA) SPEEDWAY
The Gold Cup Race of Champions was first run in 1951, at Hughes Stadium in Sacramento, California. The event was then held at West Capital Speedway until it moved to its present location—Silver Dollar Speedway.

Amazingly, some of the early races were as long as two hundred laps. They've been shortened to "only" one hundred laps since 1972. Many of the famous names that have dominated other classic events have won this one; Steve Kinser, Doug Wolfgang, Sammy Swindell, and others have all had victories in the Gold Cup Race of Champions. World of Outlaw regular Andy Hillenburg won the event in both 1994 and 1995.

MEMPHIS (TENNESSEE) MOTORSPORTS PARK
In 1991, this track made history when $65,000 went to the winner of the Fram Dash. At the time, that was the largest payout by any racing facility. The race was held at the Memphis Motorsports Park only one time (surprise—Steve Kinser won it) before it moved to Royce City, Texas.

Right: Since two refueling pit stops are required at the Little 500, there are certainly some interesting refueling arrangements. (Bill Holder)

Below, top: Andy Hillenburg (2) passes Lee Brewer, Jr. in competition at the 1995 Gold Cup race at Silver Dollar Speedway. (Donna Peter)

Below, bottom: David Steele races to victory at the 1996 Little 500 in his non-winged pavement sprinter in Anderson, Indiana. (Randy Jones)

Top left: The field lines up for a start at the Super Dirt Cup race in the Super Dirt Cup Sprint Car Classic. (First Turn)

Top right: Sprint car drivers are very accommodating of their fans. Here, one autographs a shirt. (Larry Reese)

Left: Sammy Swindell (1) and Steve Kinser (11) both pull wheelies as they pour on the coal striving for the lead position. (MSPN)

DAYTON (OHIO) SPEEDWAY

Built in 1934, the Dayton Speedway held national sprint car races for many years. All of the great sprint drivers spent time on the pavement of this high-banked, half-mile track, which ran until 1982. The site is now a landfill.

ASCOT (CALIFORNIA) PARK

This track was the home of the California Racing Association (CRA) sprint organization for many years, and the famous Don Branson was killed at Ascot in 1966. The legendary track was torn down in the 1990s, a casualty of industrial growth.

WINCHESTER (INDIANA) SPEEDWAY

Built in a cornfield by Frank Funk, the Winchester Speedway has been active since 1914, making it one of the oldest tracks in the U.S. For many years it has hosted AAA and USAC sprint cars. Known for its high banks and blazing speed, the track tests the abilities of man and machine to the ultimate.

SALEM (INDIANA) SPEEDWAY

This track was known as one of the three "hills" (the other high-banked tracks with that designation are the Dayton and Winchester Speedways). Built in 1947, the Salem Speedway has been forced to close down at times, but it became active again in the 1990s. Non-winged USAC sprint cars are still the favorite at Salem, where Rich Vogler was killed in 1990.

Opposite: Larry Rice (98), now a race announcer with ESPN, battles Jerry Weeks at the famous Terre Haute Action Track in 1976. (Ken Coles)

Opposite: Volusia County Speedway near Daytona Beach, Florida, has hosted many big sprint car races through the years. Here, Red Stauffer (2) and Ed Lynch (2L) do battle. (Phil Kunz)

Top left: Mario Andretti in the GAPCO Sprinter qualifying at Terre Haute, Indiana, in 1963. (Ken Coles)

Bottom left: Don Brown in 1969 in a roadster that he designed and built. These cars were never a threat to the uprights—especially on dirt. Unfortunately, the track at the famous high-banked Dayton Speedway is now gone. (Ken Coles)

Below: Jeff Gordon (4) and Bruce Field (85) battle each other at Salem Speedway in 1990 in USAC sprint cars. Gordon won the race. (Kevin Horcher)

DEVILS BOWL (TEXAS) SPEEDWAY

This half-mile dirt oval was built in 1973. The Devils Bowl Speedway hosts a number of large sprint car events, including the World of Outlaws.

LERNERVILLE (PENNSYLVANIA) SPEEDWAY

The present track was built by the late Don Martin after several other tracks ran under the same name. This raceway hosts a number of large sprint car events during the season.

Sprint Car Organizations

SPRINT CAR ORGANIZATION	TYPE OF SPRINTER	RACE LOCATIONS
360 Outlaw Sprint Association	limited	Kansas
All Star Circuit of Champions (ASCoC)	super	East
American Sprint Car Series (ASCS)	limited	South
Auto Value Super Sprints	super	Michigan, Indiana
Challenger Series by ASCS	limited	Ohio
Bridgeport Open-Comp Sprint Series	super	New Jersey
Cajun Sprinters Association	limited	South
Capital Promotions Hires Winged Sprints	limited	Indiana
Challenger Series by ASCS	limited	Ohio
Eastern Limited Sprints (ELS)	limited	New York
Empire Super Sprints (ESS)	limited	New York
Empire Super Sprints (ESS)	super	New York
International Motor Contest Association (IMCA)	limited	Midwest
Interstate Racing Association	super	Midwest
Keystone Auto Racing Speedways (KARS)	limited	Pennsylvania
Montana Open Wheel Racing Association	limited	Northwest
NAPA Super Sportsman Tour	econo	Pennsylvania
National Champ Racing Association (NCRA)	super/limited	Missouri, Oklahoma
Northern Auto Racing Club (NARC)	super	California
Northern Auto Racing Club	super	N. California
Northern Sprint Tour	limited	Northwest, Canada
PA Four-Cylinder Sprint Car Association	four-cylinder	Pennsylvania
Pacific Sprints	limited	California
Southern California Racing Association	super	California
Southern Ontario Sprints (SOS)	limited	Canada
Southern Outlaw Sprint Car Series	super	Alabama, Tennessee
Sprint Car Owners of Arizona	super	Arizona
Sprint Car Racing Association (SCRA)	super	West Coast
Sprints on Dirt (SOD)	limited	Michigan
Tampa Bay Auto Racing Association (TBARA)	limited	Florida
United Racing Club (URC)	limited	East
United States Auto Club (USAC)	super	East
Washington Econo Sprint Car Organization	econo	Washington, Oregon
World of Outlaws (WoO)	super	Nationwide
World Series Sprint Cars	super	Australia

Opposite: Current NASCAR Winston Cup driver Ken Schrader backs it out during a 1983 USAC sprint car race at the Terre Haute Action Track. (John Mahoney)

Right: With sprint cars, you often have to turn right to go left. (Phil Kunz)

Opposite: Aerodynamics is the name of the game with winged sprint cars. (Phil Kunz)

Sprint Car Champions

WORLD OF OUTLAWS SPRINT CAR CHAMPIONS

1978—Steve Kinser
1979—Steve Kinser
1980—Steve Kinser
1981—Sammy Swindell
1982—Sammy Swindell
1983—Steve Kinser
1984—Steve Kinser
1985—Steve Kinser
1986—Steve Kinser
1987—Steve Kinser
1988—Steve Kinser
1989—Bobby Davis, Jr.
1990—Steve Kinser
1991—Steve Kinser
1992—Steve Kinser
1993—Steve Kinser
1994—Steve Kinser
1995—Dave Blaney
1996—Mark Kinser
1997—Sammy Swindell

ALL STAR CIRCUIT OF CHAMPIONS SPRINT CAR CHAMPIONS

(There were no championships in 1971–72 or 1974–78)

1970—Ralph Quarterson
1973—Jan Opperman
1979—Dub May
1980—Bobby Allen
1981—Lee Osborne
1982—Lee Osborne
1983—Lee Osborne
1984—Fred Linder
1985—Jack Hewitt
1986—Fred Linder
1987—Joe Gaerte
1988—Joe Gaerte
1989—Robbie Stanley
1990—Terry Shephard
1991—Frankie Kerr
1992—Kevin Huntley
1993—Kevin Huntley–
        Frankie Kerr
1994—Frankie Kerr
1995—Dale Blaney
1996—Dale Blaney
1997—Frankie Kerr

USAC SPRINT CAR CHAMPIONS

(Midwest division)
1956—Pat O'Connor
1957—Elmer George
1958—Eddie Sachs
1959—Don Branson
1960—Parnelli Jones

(Eastern division)
1956—Tommy Hinnershitz
1957—Bill Randall
1958—Johnny Thomson
1959—Tommy Hinnershitz
1960—A.J. Foyt

USAC SPRINT CAR CHAMPIONS

(Midwest and Eastern divisions joined in 1961)

1961—Parnelli Jones
1962—Parnelli Jones
1963—Roger McCluskey
1964—Don Branson
1965—Johnny Rutherford
1966—Roger McCluskey
1967—Greg Weld
1968—Larry Dickson
1969—Gary Bettenhausen
1970—Larry Dickson
1971—Gary Bettenhausen
1972—Sammy Sessions
1973—Rollie Beale
1974—Pancho Carter
1975—Larry Dickson
1976—Pancho Carter
1977—Sheldon Kinser
1978—Tom Bigelow
1979—Greg Leffler
1980—Rich Vogler
1981—Sheldon Kinser
1982—Sheldon Kinser
1983—Ken Schrader
1984—Rick Hood
1985—Rick Hood
1986—Steve Butler
1987—Steve Butler
1988—Steve Butler
1989—Rich Vogler
1990—Steve Butler
1991—Robbie Stanley
1992—Robbie Stanley
1993—Robbie Stanley
1994—Doug Kalitta
1995—Tony Stewart
1996—Brian Tyler
1997—Brian Tyler

Opposite: All Star series driver Van Gurley moves to the front in a 1995 race. (Phil Kunz)

Left: The great looks of the top sprint cars are as impressive as their performance. (David Tucker)

Overleaf left: Larry Dickson at speed in Carl Gelhousen's rear-engine USAC sprint car at Winchester Speedway in 1973. Tom Sneva took over driving the car and won six feature races on pavement. (Ken Coles)

Overleaf right: USAC pavement sprinters line up for a 1993 race at Salem Speedway. (John Mahoney)

Dean Jacobs was uninjured in this spectacular 1997 crash at Eldora Speedway. (Bob Fairman)